The God Question

A Layman's Search for Proof of the Almighty

Dave Morse

WESTBOW
PRESS
A DIVISION OF THOMAS NELSON
& ZONDERVAN

WestBow Press books may be ordered through
booksellers or by contacting:

WestBow Press
A Division of Thomas Nelson & Zondervan
1663 Liberty Drive
Bloomington, IN 47403
www.westbowpress.com
1 (866) 928-1240

ISBN: 978-1-4908-7922-2 (sc)
ISBN: 978-1-4908-7923-9 (e)

Library of Congress Control Number: 2015907617

Print information available on the last page.

WestBow Press rev. date: 7/21/2015

Contents

Introduction

Is there a God out there? You know … a supreme, all-powerful being, a sovereign Creator? And if this God does exist, what kind of a deity is he? Or she? Or it?

I've learned through innumerable discussions over the years that these are questions many people would like to get sure answers to. The problem is that wherever we turn, we're given different opinions that usually only serve to confuse us further. It becomes tempting to give up the search, but we shouldn't—because the answers to these questions hold the key to unlocking our very identity.

As a person of faith who has believed in the Eternal my whole life, I found myself caught off guard one day when a colleague of mine challenged me to prove it. I knew this was no small task, but my competitive nature wouldn't allow me to back down from the challenge, so off I went.

This book summarizes my journey through the disciplines of science, religion, philosophy, and history in an effort to find evidence—no, proof—of a Creator.

I hold no theological degrees or church offices, hopefully allowing my starting point to be free of denominational shackles.

My desire is that this account will help seekers sort out some of the mess that has been created over the centuries regarding this essential issue. And who knows—maybe they'll even find a few answers. Happy reading!

CHAPTER 1

The Problem

Ever since I was a child, I've been fascinated with how things work. Whether the object is mechanical or biological, simple or complex, it doesn't matter. Take our bodies, for example. Did you know that the average body contains over sixty-thousand miles of blood vessels? That's long enough to wrap more than twice around the earth's equator![1] Yet our hearts are strong enough to pump our blood in a complete circuit around our body in just over a minute—totaling over one thousand times each day.[2] Just think about that for a moment!

The hydrochloric acid in our stomachs is actually strong enough to eat through iron, but remarkably, it doesn't hurt the stomach wall. This is thanks to a film of mucus that protects it.[3] This lining replaces half a

[1] Christopher Maynard, Janet DeSaulles, and Hazel Songhurst, *How Your Body Works* (New York: Smithmark Publishers, 1998), 15.

[2] Editors of Time Life Books, *Mysteries of the Human Body—Library of Curious & Unusual Facts* (Alexandria, VA: Time-Life Books, 1992), 9.

[3] Isaac Asimov, *Isaac Asimov's Book of Facts—1981 Edition* (New York: Bell Publishing Co./Red Dembner Enterprises Corp., 1979), 324.

million cells a minute to keep up with those cells lost to the hydrochloric acid.[4] That's half a million cells *a minute*. Incredible!

Our bones are amazing too. Did you know that some of our bones can support more weight than granite and that when pulled end from end, they can endure ten thousand to twenty thousand pounds of force per square inch? In order to keep from damaging fragile tissue, though, our bones are incredibly lightweight. In fact, the entire skeleton of a 160-pound body weighs only about twenty-nine pounds.[5]

Then there's the human brain. Every second, around four billion nerve impulses fire back and forth between our brains' left and right hemispheres, and some one hundred thousand different chemical reactions occur, forming our thoughts, emotions, and actions.[6] If it weren't true, this would seem impossible. In addition, over a lifetime of seventy years, our memories hold at least one hundred trillion bits of information. The entire *Encyclopedia Britannica* is only two hundred million bits. This translates into ten thousand bits of information stored per brain cell.[7]

When my head gets bigger than it should, details like these help me to realize I don't know as much as I think I do. While these facts about our bodies are staggering at

---

[4] Editors, *Mysteries of the Human Body,* 17.

[5] Ibid., 28.

[6] Neil McAleer, *The Body Almanac—Mind Boggling Facts About Today's Human Body and High-Tech Medicine* (Garden City, NY: Doubleday & Company, Inc., 1985), 2.

[7] Ibid., 6, 18.

the least, they raise one important question: Where did we come from? As one who has always believed there's an artist behind our design, my immediate thought has consistently been … God!

The Almighty?

The notion of a Supreme Ruler, a Divine Creator, or an Omnipotent Being has spawned the devotion of billions of people over the millennia. Many of these adherents to the Almighty give logical reasons for their beliefs, coupled with accounts of the miraculous and a deep spiritual presence in their lives. At the same time, there are just as many individuals who firmly declare that no such being exists, and they back their statements with logic and scientific evidence that's just as compelling as the accounts of believers.

So which is it? Is there a God out there or not? And if there is, what kind of God is he? Or she? Or it? It seems as though every believing person I meet gives me a different description of this eternal deity, and every nonbeliever provides a different reason for his or her convictions. So who has the answers? Who can we listen to so we can get to the bottom of this? Does anyone really know?

....

"How can I know who's right?" He asked.

....

I'm reminded of a situation I found myself in a few years ago. A coworker and I were driving to a workshop one morning when the topic of religion came up. As I began to share some of my thoughts, he suddenly stopped me and countered with a series of tough questions. "How do you know your beliefs are right? Others share the same amount of faith, conviction, and devotion as you, but in a completely different religion. How can I know who's right?" he asked. "Also, each religion has its own holy book that it claims comes from God. How can I know which, if any, of them truly is of God?"

My friend's challenge somewhat unnerved me. I knew what he was really saying behind the questions: "If you claim God is out there, show him to me. Prove it." This was an honest challenge that caused me to search for evidence and answers to the questions many people have.

My friend didn't want to play around with this. He didn't want me to simply share my ideas, insights, experiences, or beliefs. He wanted to know the facts. Is God out there or not? If so, which god is the real God? Any of them? All of them? Can we know which religions are human-made and which are from God? Are any of them right? It seems like all religious people have failed to live up to the standards of their faith. Whom can we trust for answers?

Some of us never voice these questions as we have people around us who consider these kinds of inquiries as irreverent and label them as taboo. In strict religions or cultures, others may even shun us for asking. But it doesn't stop us from wondering. Deep inside, something stirs and is hungry, wanting to be fed the truth. But what is that truth? Can it ever be known? It all seems so confusing sometimes.

I believed in God, and I knew why, but could I find the kind of proof about this being that my friend sought? I now wanted to know the answers to his questions about God as well. I began searching. I was also curious about what other people thought, so I started asking around. In fact, I've spoken with so many people about this topic that I have lost count.

Foundational Thoughts

I've spoken with friends, relatives, neighbors, coworkers, and complete strangers. I've talked to them in cars, boats, and planes. We've met in stores, homes, prisons, hospitals, restaurants, and churches and on the street, college campuses, and even the sides of mountains. There are some interesting people out there, with an equal number of interesting thoughts on the subject, so where do we begin to find the evidence we seek in such a diverse world? Does absolute truth on this matter really exist?

Maybe it's just the practical New England blood that flows through me, but it seems that a set of truths exists about everything. Yes, there are some who question truth to the degree that they've tried to convince me the chair I'm sitting on doesn't actually exist. Or that it really isn't a chair. I'm sorry, but I can't help wondering why I don't find myself sprawled on the ground if this is true. In my finite mind, the article exists, and it's of the design known to all humankind as a chair. All the other items that look like it and serve the same function also exist—and I refer to them as chairs as well.

I believe that a set of truths exists about everything, even about God. The fact that I believe we have a Creator doesn't mean there is one. Likewise, if I subscribe to an atheistic view, it wouldn't mean there definitely isn't a Creator. The real question in many people's minds is whether solid evidence can be found to support either idea. As I mentioned previously, this book summarizes what the disciplines of science, religion, and philosophy have to say on the topic. It also details what I have found through my own search.

....

**If a God exists who wants to be
known by humans, he will
reveal himself in a way that
stands out, that is obvious,
and that clearly shows who he is.**

....

I should reveal here at the beginning that I've made a small handful of presuppositions within my thought process that seem logical to me. These are as follows:

1. *If no God exists, no evidence will be found of such a being.*
2. *If a God exists who has no interest in humankind, some evidence may or may not be found, but I would have no real interest in him, either.*

3. *If a God exists who wants to be known by humans, he will reveal himself in a way that stands out, that is obvious, and that clearly shows who he is.*

4. *Truth about this matter exists, whatever that truth is. We may conclude at the end that the truth cannot be known, but that is different from the truth not existing.*

Truth

So God is either out there, or he's not. Which is it? One of these statements is the truth, and one is not. Either of these statements could be true, but both can't be—and that's the problem. You see, that means some of the people I've spoken with are right and some are wrong. And some may be partly right, but that means they're also partly wrong.

Most of these people came from different religious backgrounds, including atheism. Of those individuals who believe God exists, many of them had different ideas about who he is, based on their background. But again, despite what our accepting culture desires, not all can be right. But not all are necessarily wrong either.

Many I have met quote the popular adage, "As many rivers flow to the ocean, so all religions flow to God." Some even say that no religion or personal belief system is completely right but that all contain partial truth. Is this true? Does it matter which religion we choose to follow to "find" God? Aren't we all part of God anyway? Do I even need to subscribe to any particular set of doctrines? Can't I find God on my own?

If God exists, it would be nice if he'd reveal himself (or herself) and clear up this confusion. Some state that he has already revealed himself—but how? Everyone seems to have a different answer. How do we know what's right? Whom should we listen to? Am I supposed to live a certain way? If so, is the life I'm living good enough for the God who may be out there? What's the purpose for your life and mine? For humanity as a whole? Does any of this even matter?

CHAPTER 2

Beginning the Search

Tracking down the kind of proof people desire about God has its challenges. I have a number of friends who tell me that their communion with the Almighty is found in the chapel of the outdoors—usually with a fishing rod in hand. This seems like a good place to start, as most religions and philosophies in the world tie God to nature in some way. They state he either reveals himself through nature's splendor or his spirit indwells nature's various creatures. A good number of the people I spoke with believe they can sense God's presence in some way through the natural world.

> Nature is too thin a screen; the glory of the omnipresent God bursts through everywhere.
> —Ralph Waldo Emerson[8]

---

[8] Bob Kelly, *Worth Repeating: More Than 5000 Classic and Contemporary Quotes* (Grand Rapids, MI: Kregel Publications, 2003), 241.

> Earth's crammed with heaven,
> And every common bush afire with God.
> —Elizabeth Barrett Browning[9]

The design and beauty of a flower, the intelligence of the dolphin, the majesty of the eagle, the artistry of a sunset, and the vastness of the oceans all point in various ways to a God or Great Spirit for so many people. However, for a good number of others, these all point to evidence of anything but a God. They feel it's impossible for just one being to create anything as complex and detailed as what we find in our world—not to mention the rest of the universe.

Because so many of the people I spoke with referred to the influence of science, I felt it was prudent to expand my search for information about God to include not just nature but everything that's studied in the physical world by this discipline. Maybe this would help to uncover some evidence about whether or not this being exists, and if he does exist, some insight into his character might also be revealed. Therefore, as I examined the full realm of nature, I was challenged to consider more than just what our senses, or even our spirits, reveal to us.

We need to also bear in mind the complexities of the human brain, the migratory senses of birds, the power of quasars, the balance of an ecosystem, the design of a cell, or even the structure of water. Did these things come or evolve into being through a complex natural process, or are they the work of a Master Craftsman?

---

[9]   Mary Rosenda Sullivan, *Structure in Language and Literature* (New York: W. H. Sadlier, 1965), 59.

Maybe taking this look at the entire natural world through the eyes of science can help us learn something about this seemingly evasive deity. Science is a powerful discipline that provides us with new breakthroughs in understanding on nearly a daily basis.

The Scientific Method

Let's consider for a moment the foundation of modern science—the scientific method. This process is one of the best-devised systems for gaining knowledge and understanding about the universe we live in that has ever existed. Though simple and logical enough to be understood by grade-school children around the world, the use of the scientific method has been instrumental in unlocking cures for diseases, developing new forms of transportation, improving agricultural production, and even exploring the reaches of our galaxy.

While it was extremely valuable on many levels, my examination of the realm of science led me to recognize that the effectiveness of this orderly process may be limited in some applications. You see, the scientific method is a procedure for experimentation that involves constructing a hypothesis that is then tested. The resulting data is analyzed, and a conclusion about the hypothesis is drawn. To succeed, this whole practice first requires the step of observation, though, thus possibly revealing its limitations in a search for the Almighty.

Has God, if he exists, chosen to remain unobservable, at least from a scientific perspective? Maybe he has, or maybe he hasn't. Many contend that God dwells in a spiritual realm—a realm entirely different from the physical realm we live in. Does this mean that science is of no help to us here? Let's look further.

The Voices of Science

I learned that a number of members of the scientific community infer that though direct observation of this being may not be available, enough indirect evidence has been gathered to support some final conclusions about God. Some of these scientists state that no God exists because pieces of this body of evidence suggest that the universe was formed on its own, with no divine intervention. They assert that this occurred when an extremely dense microparticle exploded billions of years ago. Within this particle, only a couple of nature's elements existed, but there was enough heat to create the rest of the elements after the explosion occurred. This blast led to the creation of billions of planets and stars, some of which are incredibly large. The star Antares, for example, is many thousands of times larger than earth. In addition, all of the biological agents and physical components of the universe developed over time, and eventually life itself appeared, followed by instincts, adaptive abilities, and intelligence.

While this conclusion is worth consideration, other members of the same scientific community relay that one must make a poor and incomplete application of the scientific method to reach this conclusion, based on the limited body of evidence that has been observed. They testify that no determination about the existence or absence of a Creator God can be made. Much more testing and research needs to be done, and many more pieces of evidence need to be found. Until then, they declare, the notion of this dense microparticle remains a hypothesis.

Interestingly, I found that while these two factions plant their flags at opposite ends of this existential matter, yet still a third group of scientists attempts to reconcile the two views. They state that this theory of the formation of the universe proves both the existence of God and the manner in which he created the universe. In other words, God exists, and the big bang theory explains the method God used when he created everything.

....

> **The scientific community itself can't agree on what inferences should be made from our current collection of data.**

....

So what did I learn from the scientific community about the notion of whether or not God exists, based on the study of the origin of the universe? Though it may be frustrating, it seems to me that no concrete conclusions can be drawn, as the scientific community itself can't agree on what inferences should be made from our current collection of data.

Other Scientific Findings

When I took a look at our own origin, I discovered that similar arguments have been made concerning science's claims about God and the theory of evolution. Some scientists look at the evidence offered by certain fossils and conclude that no Creator God exists, as all creatures evolved. Other scientists state that the fossil evidence is incomplete and that no conclusions can therefore be drawn. Yet still others insist that the fossil evidence reveals the very method that a God used to create man—through an evolutionary process. Again, we're left unable to draw any concrete conclusions about God's existence, as equally logical-sounding arguments can be made by each camp.

Some scientific news I read a while ago expressed that the mapping of the human genome was proving to be one of the greatest scientific accomplishments of this young millennium. Interestingly, it also provided us with a current example of the scientific community's debate between advocates of the theory of evolution and supporters of the concept of intelligent design.

In February of 2001, two separate articles appeared in different publications within two days of each other. Each author was apparently unaware of the other article's existence. These articles responded to the mapping of the human genome, which had been completed only months before and was jointly announced by the publicly funded Human Genome Project and the privately funded Celera Genomics Corporation of Rockville, Maryland.

In the article appearing in the *San Francisco Chronicle*, Dr. Gene Myers, the scientist whose computer program unraveled the genome sequence, was quoted. Dr. Myers stated that the genome sequence is complex and seems as though it was designed, with an intelligence behind it.[10]

Dr. Arthur Caplan, director of the Center for Bioethics at the University of Pennsylvania in Philadelphia, provided a different perspective on the matter. In his article he emphatically stated that the genome fully supports Darwin's theory of evolution.[11]

So there it was, staring back at me. Two scientists working on the same project seemed to draw two different conclusions. My search revealed that scientists from all disciplines have been divided over the issues of evolution, creation, the formation of the universe, and intelligent design for decades—and the debate continues today.

Many scientists have published journal articles and books on the subject. In some situations, individuals who are quoted in one place as sounding supportive of evolutionary theory or the big bang theory can be found making statements in other places that sound supportive of creation or intelligent design and vice versa.

. . . .

Whether one adheres to the intelligent design perspective or to the big bang/evolution theories, both parties rely on faith.

. . . .

---

[10] Tom Abate, "Human Genome Map Has Scientists Talking About the Divine," *San Francisco Chronicle* (February 19, 2001).

[11] Arthur L. Caplan, "Darwin Vindicated!" MSNBC www.msnbc.com (February 21, 2001) and *The American Journal of Bioethics* www.bioethics.net (February 21, 2001).

It seems to me that these inconsistencies of viewpoint at various stages of individual scientists' thoughts illustrate the fact that we cannot make conclusive statements, based on evidence gathered and processed to date, about the existence or absence of a supreme being. Perhaps the most revealing perspective I've heard is one spoken by a number of individuals I've encountered in various scientific and academic forums.

These individuals note that whether one adheres to the intelligent design perspective or to the big bang/evolution theories, both parties rely on faith. One has faith in a being who is not directly observable and who supersedes the laws of science. The other has faith in scientific theories that do not yet have sufficient evidence to support them.

What Did I Learn?

Making sense of matters that involve physical evidence are challenging enough. Adding the intangibles of our world makes the task facing our scientific community even more difficult. For instance, where do animals acquire their instincts? How do birds know where to migrate? How is a newborn baby born with the intuition to suckle? Mothers don't have to teach this to a healthy child. How about the source of life? When you swat a mosquito, all of its parts are still there, but there is no life left in it. We could rebuild our squashed nemesis, but we can't infuse it with life. Where does that life come from? Where does it go? Do we have spirits and souls, or are we just assemblies of matter? What happens at the point of death? Is there an afterlife? Science, as a discipline, has thus far been unable to find answers to these questions.

So has science failed us? Certainly not! The discipline of science has provided mankind with understanding about a great many things and has allowed for the development of numerous beneficial technologies. However, my search through science showed me that concerning the matter of the existence of a God, the boundaries of science have simply been overreached.

The scientific method is limited by the requirement that sufficient observation and experimentation be completed before a conclusion can be drawn. It seems the very nature of a God removes this being from the grasp of science and from many of our own inferences about him gained through our personal experiences in nature, as well. The close scientific examination of nature and the universe has led to many irreconcilable theories—with the involvement of a God being only one of them.

My quest led me to discover that science, due to its limitations, is unable to provide ample proof of the existence of a divine Creator and is simultaneously unable to eliminate the possibility of his existence as well. Therefore, it seems to me that science finds itself outside of its capability in this matter and unable to help the seeker of concrete, genuine truth concerning the existence of a God. Besides, if science and nature did point us to God, which one is it—the Muslim one, the Christian one, a Native American one, or one of the many Hindu gods? Is this God still involved with mankind or not? Does he take a personal interest in us, or are our circumstances designed simply for his amusement? Or his experimentation? Or something else entirely?

CHAPTER 3

How about Religion?

The realms of nature and science seem to leave us with more questions than answers, so I figured the next logical place to look for insight about God would be the world of religion. After all, who knows more about God than religious people?

The problem with searching through the world's religions quickly becomes evident—which religion do we turn to for truth? I found even people who are already grounded in a particular religion or faith occasionally ponder this issue.

Despite sporadic efforts to create some unity and cooperation between each other, the religions of the world are philosophically and doctrinally opposed to each other. As a result, it is impossible for all of them to be right. One religion holds to a triune God, and another teaches that there is only a singular God. A third religion believes in one unknowable God who takes many forms, while yet another states there are many gods to follow— each with a different personality and role. To add to the confusion, most religions have their own divinely inspired texts, none of which fully agree with each other, if they even agree at all. Some teach about a spiritual life after death, and some teach about a physical life after death. Some believe that *sunyata* (void, emptiness, nonexistence) is every man's origin and demise, while others promote human transcendence, tying man to the world of *samsara* or the cycle of rebirth.

To further convolute the matter, I found that many different denominations exist within the world's major religions, leaving seekers utterly disillusioned and somewhat jaded. Islam, for instance, is separated into five major divisions: Sunni Muslims, Shi'ite Muslims, the Wahhabi sect, the Suffi sect, and Bahaiism. Buddhism contains three chief movements: Theravada, Mahayana, and Vajrayana. Hinduism includes over a thousand major denominations, based on which Hindu god you choose to follow.

The Christian church is no different. It is divided into the two major branches of Catholicism and Protestantism, and each of these branches contains many denominations.

The Catholic Church states that it is only one denomination; however, a number of divisions have been spawned from the Catholic Church over the years that are still quite active today. Some of these divisions include the Byzantine Catholics, Roman Catholics, Anglican Catholics, Free Catholics, and the Mariavite Church.

The Protestant branch of the Christian church also contains many divisions, including Presbyterians, Baptists, Pentecostals, Wesleyans, Methodists, Calvinists, Lutherans, Anglicans, etc. Taking a look at just the Baptist denomination alone reveals a large number of sub-denominations, including American Baptists, Reformed Baptists, Independent Baptists, Progressive Baptists, United Baptists, Grace Baptists, Primitive Baptists, Southern Baptists, Free Will Baptists, Liberty Baptists, and Fundamental Baptists.

....

At some point, one has to question how much of this is God-made and how much is fabricated by the mind and will of man.

....

What a mess! To the sincere seeker of truth about God, the claims of religion must appear ridiculous. It seems to me that at some point, one has to question how much of this is God-made and how much is fabricated by the mind and will of man.

It Gets Worse

To make matters even more confusing, I realized none of these major religions can be readily dismissed as completely without value. Each religion has at least a handful of doctrines that seem logical and reasonable, providing practical guidance for living life reasonably and successfully with others on this planet. These doctrines even give convincing-sounding insight into what happens after death. Each religion requires an element of faith (even atheism), and each has had its share of successes and failures. Every one of the major religions seems reasonable in some regards and extreme or fanatical in others.

In other words, every religion has its own positions on spiritual matters, and very few of the views of one religion match those of another (though just enough are similar to keep things confusing). As an example, I took just one topic—the identity of God—and compared the views of a number of the world's major religions on the issue. One would think that religions may differ on minor issues, but surely something as significant as the identity of God should serve as a common thread. Here are the definitions each of the religions gives:

Bahai faith:	One God who can't be known but by his attributes; all religions understand part of him.
Buddhism:	Man created God in response to fear and frustration.
Chinese religion:	Worship a variety of deities (*shen*) found in nature. Also, deify some people, national heroes and ancestors, among others.
Christianity:	One God who is a Trinity of Father, Son, and Holy Spirit.
Confucianism:	Tian—similar to Tao and multiple deities (*shen*).
Deism:	One Creator God (no Trinity) who leaves the world alone to run by the laws of nature.

Hinduism:	Various sects with many gods and goddesses.
Islam:	One God, Allah. Nothing in creation resembles him. No Trinity.
Jehovah's Witnesses:	One God, Jehovah. No Trinity. Christ was created by God; the Holy Spirit is an impersonal force.
Judaism:	One God, Yahweh. Holy Spirit distinct from Yahweh.
Mormonism:	God the Father, the Son, Jesus Christ, and the Holy Spirit are three separate individual beings who are united in purpose, will, and other attributes.
New Age:	All religions lead to the same single source of divine energy.
Shinto:	Various gods and goddesses (*kami*).
Sikhism:	One Creator ("Ik Onkar") who is everywhere and is the only truth.
Taoism:	The universe comes from the Tao, and there are many deities with specific roles.

Every one of the major world religions in this list claims millions of followers. If a concept as significant as the identity of God can't be agreed upon, just think of the confusion over matters such as the afterlife, the involvement of God with man, man's purpose and role, the relationship between the spiritual and physical worlds, the claims of prophets, sacred writings, and the existence and roles of angels and demons. My head began to spin as soon as I started reading on these subjects.

I've been asked more than once about the Indian parable of the blind men and the elephant in relation to God and religion. You've probably heard it before. In the story, six blind men are asked to describe an elephant based on the part of the elephant they touch. One man feels the trunk and says an elephant is like a tree branch. Another man touches an ear and describes the elephant as being like a fan. The other four state that an elephant is like a tree trunk (leg), a rope (tail), a solid pipe (tusk), and a wall (belly). While each man describes the elephant differently, they are all really describing parts of the same thing. If the men can learn to put aside their differences and cooperate and communicate with each other, they will all eventually gain a full understanding of what an elephant looks like.

Does this Indian parable describe the role of religion in the world? Could God have chosen to show himself to mankind by sharing pieces of himself through each major religion? Will we never truly get a clear picture of who God is unless we take this approach and view each religion as holding a valid piece of the puzzle?

I agree that we all should strive for unity and cooperation with each other. Nearly every religion in the world values loving one another and living in peace with each other as basic tenets. As I studied each religion, though, I realized that this parable does not describe the way any God could have revealed himself to us. What the world's religions bring to the table is entirely different from what the parts of the elephant bring.

In the parable, there is only one tail, with only one description for that tail. There is also only one trunk, one belly, and so forth. You can put their descriptions all together and get one understanding of what an elephant is. If we applied this concept to God, we would focus on his various components, such as his nature, his purpose, his role in creation, his expectations of us, etc. The problem is that the world's religions bring us dozens of descriptions of his nature and purpose, scores of ideas about his role in creation, and even more thoughts about his expectations of us. And few are similar. When assembled together, these assumptions produce a nearly countless number of versions of God, thus leaving us where we began— wondering who God is or if he's even there at all.

My search for truth about God in the realm of religion has led to another unresolved end. It seems to me that not much more can be said about this subject as a means to finding absolute truth about God. There are concurrently too many similarities and too many differences between the religions of the world to be able to draw any conclusions about God that can be confirmed as truth. It also appears there is far too much interjection of human thought into religion as a whole to be able to separate out idealized fabrications from truth. To put it simply, we are left not knowing whom to believe.

....

It's unfortunate that religion brings more confusion than help to the one who seeks concrete truth about God.

....

Does this mean that the world's religions are devoid of value? Not at all. They provide societies with a foundation of values and morality that laws alone cannot offer. They also get people to think about the possibility of God, which can lead us to wrestle with our origin and the implications thereof. It's unfortunate, then, that religion—the very convention that is meant to reveal God to us—as a whole brings more confusion than help to the one who seeks concrete truth about God.

CHAPTER 4

Can Philosophy Help?

How many philosophers does it take to change a light bulb? Three—one to change it and two to stand around arguing over whether the light bulb exists!

For millennia, man has pondered questions of self-realization, purpose, our relationship to the universe, and the existence and role of a supreme being. Unlike scientific thought, which is restricted to pursuing the observable, the discipline of philosophical thinking can tackle the intangible issues of life, though the two disciplines may intersect with each other at times. It seemed plausible that perhaps through philosophy I could gain some logic-based evidence that might provide the understanding about the Almighty that so many seek.

Many philosophers over the centuries have produced insights about God. Some of these philosophers are well known, and some are not. These insights about God have evolved over time, and while some thoughts have overlapped with others, a number of ideas have been original and unique.

I learned that one traditional philosophy concerning the existence of God goes as follows: *When one considers the universe—everything from the tiny cells in our skin to the uniqueness of the bodies in our solar system—one discovers that it is extremely complex. Because of its complexity, it would be impossible for the universe to have simply formed by chance; therefore, it must have been created by a Grand Designer.* Of course, this notion has been countered by an equally popular and compelling idea: *Nothing this vast in scope and complex in detail could have possibly been created by any one entity. No being could exist who is powerful and intelligent enough to do this. Besides, who would have created him?*

Rene Descartes, who is most remembered for declaring *cogito ergo sum*, or "I think, therefore I am," conjectured further on the matter of the existence of God. Based on the knowledge of his own existence, Descartes determined that he could not have caused himself to exist because he was an imperfect being and thus was incapable of such a feat. If he did not cause himself, then something else must have caused his existence. No matter what that something else was, Descartes surmised, something caused it to exist as well. This continuity of cause keeps working backward and must end at some point. At that ending point, one will discover it ends with God—the perfect, all-powerful being who caused himself into existence.

One common argument made to counter Descartes's writings is that if God is truly an all-powerful and thus infinite being, then he would have no need to create anything as he would already have everything. Creating something would define God as being finite; therefore, no God would ever have had a need to cause the existence of anything else that would eventually lead to causing Descartes's existence.

These are just a few of the many ideas that have been bantered around for centuries about the Almighty. The philosophical arguments for and against the existence of God are overwhelming and can be confusing and difficult to follow. The overriding philosophy of this modern age is the concept that the existence of God can be neither proved nor disproved. I found the popularity of this notion became confirmed through the many discussions I held with individuals from every walk of life.

The Philosophy Today

Among those who do believe that the Eternal exists, I've found one prevailing philosophy of our era that is frequently applied to our understanding of who God is. This philosophy holds that just as we each have our own views and beliefs concerning political issues, moral issues, personal decisions, and even legal issues, we can each hold different views of who God is and all simultaneously be right. In other words, it doesn't matter what you believe about God; it's a personal matter, and if it works for you, then it is right.

So what about this view of God? Many have told me they want nothing to do with formal, organized religion. These individuals feel it only gets in the way of a wholesome relationship with their Creator. They have their own personal relationships with God, and they let me know that no one had better question anything about it. Just because their God may be different from everyone else's doesn't mean they're wrong.

So I wondered, what about this? Is it possible for a God to alter his identity, his approach, and his standards to accommodate every person who desires a "personalized" relationship with him? By nature, God is capable of anything, so I realized the real question is whether it is logical or even practical for him to become individualized in this manner.

If God were to allow every person to have a unique view of him, accompanied by a unique set of standards and values, what would the result be? It seems as though it would be the discord, confusion, doubt, guilt, and hatred that fills our planet today. Many of the problems found in our world over the centuries have stemmed from the wide variety of beliefs that exist regarding who we are in relation to a Creator. It seems logical to me that if a God exists, if we all have a similar understanding of who he is, and if he provided one set of standards and values for all of us to follow, we would experience much more unity in this world.

What if a God exists, though, who valued his individual relationships with us more than any set of standards? In other words, couldn't God relate to each of us differently instead of presenting himself the same to all of us? What if he didn't mind a little disorder? Well, this is possible, but I think before I could paint this kind of picture of him, I would need to consider what this God has done.

The God of Order

When I look at the world and everything in it, I become amazed at the variety and the complexity of detail that surrounds me. Simultaneously, though, I can't help but notice the symbiotic relationships that permeate nature, keeping everything in balance.

....

**If this world is created, then
the one who created it
is incredibly organized.**

....

Any significant catalyst that would throw this interdependence of organisms and species out of equilibrium could cause the world to change in a cataclysmic fashion. If this world is created, then the one who created it is incredibly organized. True chaos and disorder would be entirely against his nature (even the "chaos" observed in some aspects of nature and the universe seems to be held within parameters of order).

If we are living in a created universe, then it was created by a God of order and definition. The balance of things is precise—so precise that even the occasional imbalances that arise can be assimilated. Therefore, it seems logical that such a God would never propagate a situation that would lead to turmoil; consequently, he would never reveal himself in a different manner to different people, as this would be contrary to his nature. He would present himself the same to everyone, with the same set of standards, values, and morals for all of us to follow together.

I'm becoming more conscious of what a strange breed we are! If we believe a Creator is out there, then why aren't we seeking information from him about who he is? If he's not the one giving us each different, personalized views of himself, then who is? It seems to me that only one answer remains—it is we who are doing this.

....

We are creating God in our image.

....

Why are we placing our own values on him? From a standpoint of truth-seeking through philosophical means, this makes no sense. We all become upset when people describe us according to their own ideas as opposed to who we actually are! Ultimately we are creating God in our image. Instead, if we really want to know the Maker of the universe, I think the opposite should be occurring.

The created are trying to become the creators. God, if you're there, forgive us for our selfishness and nearsightedness. We should be seeking you, not making you. What a mess we've made of this world and the lives you've given us.

Friends, I have believed all along that somewhere a set of truth exists about God—about his existence or his absence, about his nature, about his amount of involvement or noninvolvement with man, about his degree of participation or absence concerning creation, about his personality, about what he expects and doesn't expect of us, about what he values, and about what his standards are. Many have told me that they want to find the evidence that defines these truths. They don't want to simply hear various individuals' opinions on these matters. As I previously mentioned, I found it's impossible for every religion to be a valid route to finding God, as the religions of the world are philosophically and ideologically opposed to each other. In the same way, it is impossible for each of us as individuals to have conflicting ideas about the nature of God and for all of us to be right. Someone has to be wrong. Some religion has to be wrong. Some philosophies have to be wrong. Some of us are wrong.

If sufficient evidence is found that clarifies that God really doesn't exist, then the truth of the matter is that there is no God, and all religions and people who believe in him are wrong. If the evidence reveals that God is a female, then all who believe he is a male are wrong. If it shows that God created man in his own image, then all of the evolutionists are wrong. If we discover that people go through a cycle of reincarnation, then all of the Baptists are wrong.

....

**If God does exist, only he knows
the real truth about himself.**

....

If God actually does exist, though, then only he knows the real truth about himself. It seems to me that it is reasonable for us to let him tell us what that truth is. It seems sensible that we need to get past the notion that all ideas about God are okay. I may believe he is only a

God of love who doesn't hold people accountable for their actions. Based on this belief, I may live my life licentiously. If I am wrong, though, then I may find myself being held accountable for my decisions and actions.

On the other hand, I may live my life according to a set of standards that I believe God established. If in actuality no God exists, then I have perhaps lost out on the opportunity to take a path in life that I could have otherwise had.

One thing is for sure—many ideas exist about God. These philosophies frequently oppose each other, in the same way the religions of the world oppose each other. As a result, I found that my search for the truth about God cannot be found through the discipline of philosophical thinking either. I wonder, could this perhaps be due to the fact that finite, limited minds are trying to understand a being who is infinite in nature? Are we trying to wrap our minds around a concept that is unfathomable?

I believe our philosophical thoughts are all grounded in our limited experiences in one way or another, no matter how hard we try to think outside of them. This part of my search has led me to conclude that the concept of God is too vast for us to gain a full understanding of through a philosophical approach. No matter how intelligent we are, our minds are still factually and experientially too limited.

Now What?

Science, religion, and philosophy all fell short for me as venues through which I could learn the truth about God.

The ramifications of this truth are important for all of us, though, so I needed to continue my search elsewhere for the evidence so many told me they seek. But where? What was left? Who was left? If God exists, we would really need him to reveal to us some truth about himself. If no God exists, however, then no God-imparted truth will ever be found.

As I shared previously, if a God exists who is not concerned with the affairs of mankind, some truth of him may be found, though it is not likely. But if a God exists who is involved in his creation, maybe I could find evidence of him in the pages of history. Maybe he has given us some revelations of who he is—and maybe even of what he is up to.

CHAPTER 5

One Man

In my quest, I had reached the point of realizing that the conclusions drawn by science, religion, and philosophy are too inconsistent to provide us with the answers we seek about God, and I found myself slightly unsettled by this. After all, where could I go now? Would I ever be able to find the answers that would solidify my faith and answer the questions my friend and others had?

I remembered the old adage that in order to pick something up, sometimes I first have to let go of the thing I'm already holding. Maybe I wasn't out of options after all. Maybe there was still something out there for me to pick up. Really, all I had done so far was to let go of the limited understanding I had been holding onto all along.

After studying science, religion, and philosophy for the answers, I reached the conclusion that if we're fortunate enough to have a God who is interested in man, then just maybe we can find times in history in which he revealed himself—or at least knowledge about himself—to us. If not, then I would need to really start questioning what I believed and why. So to the history books I went!

A Historical Anomaly

As I labored through my review of the annals of history, I uncovered a number of situations in which men laid claim to having had extraordinary contact with God. These men eventually received the labels of *prophet*, *saint*, or *guru*, or they received some other significant-sounding title. Several of these men eventually became founders of major world religions, while others founded lesser religions or built local followings around their teachings.

While these individuals promoted different ideas and had varying degrees of impact on humanity, one consistency is found among them. Their personal revelations—either from God, about God, from an angel, on scrolls, on golden plates, or in a vision of some sort—were all received in private. No one else received a similar revelation, and no one else witnessed these interactions between God and man. In other words, there was no affirmation or confirmation from a third party. No one else saw the scrolls or tablets, or heard the voice, or saw the vision.

....

**If a God wanted to send a message
to us, he would send it
in a way that caused people to
know, without a doubt,
that the message came from him.**

....

While the founders of major world religions deserve respect for their contributions to history, the circumstances surrounding the personal nature of their revelations leave the seeker of truth about God at a loss. Without witnesses or some other sort of proof, which of these great religious figures can the seeker turn to? As I alluded to already, it seems to me that if a God wanted to send a message to us, he would send it in a way that caused people to know, without a doubt, that the message came from him. Instead, nothing accompanied the revelations received by these men that transcended human ability, and there was no divine event that anyone else could witness. The honest seeker wonders what separates the testimony of these individuals from the testimony of anyone else who states he's received a revelation from God.

Once again I realized we are left wondering whom we can believe. Each of these men's messages contradicts the others on various levels, so clearly not all of them can be correct. Also, none of these individuals did anything superhuman or miraculous that caused them to stand out from any of the others. None of them, that is, until I dug further and found out there is one extraordinary exception—an individual who was there in front of me all along. History provides us with one man who actually does stand out as someone no one had ever seen the likes of before or since!

The One Man

It seems logical that if a God wanted to reveal himself to mankind, he would do so in some fashion that would cause people to realize that he was the one bringing the message. In other words, he wouldn't do it in secret, and he wouldn't reveal himself only to one person. He would reveal himself publically, and it would be obvious that it was God who was being revealed. He should be fully capable of doing this if he wants. After all, he's God—right?

About two thousand years ago, a man walked the earth for a short period of time who made extraordinary—even potentially blasphemous—claims about himself. He made frequent references to his relationship with a Creator God, and supernatural signs and miracles that far surpassed any human ability followed him. Everything he did was witnessed by at least his followers and usually by large crowds of people. By the time his life on earth was done, hundreds of thousands of people had watched this man and witnessed firsthand the supernatural events that surrounded him.[12] This man is Jesus Christ of Nazareth.

Some Transparency

I would like to pause at this point in the story for a moment to share some candid thoughts. Since I have revealed that the apparent conclusion of my search is Jesus Christ, some readers may conclude that I held this understanding all along. It can appear that I never searched for answers at all but simply constructed this story as a means to introduce the Christian gospel message.

---

[12] Based on records of the local population at the time of Christ made by Tacitus and Josephus.

Please understand, dear reader, that when I reached this point in my search, I was taken completely by surprise. Did I have faith in Jesus Christ? Yes. Did I believe that Jesus is God incarnate? Yes. Did I believe that Jesus came to earth, among other reasons, to reveal God to us? Again, yes. What I never saw in all of this, though, is that when the pieces of Jesus' life are all joined together, the picture that is formed provides the very proof of a Creator that I was looking for! The moment I realized this, my eyes opened, and my faith was taken to a new level. Somehow I had missed this previously.

Prior to coming upon this understanding, I had placed my faith in Christ based on individual events in his life. I had never taken everything about Christ and weighed all of it together. Once I did this, all I had trusted before became certain for me, and the proof of God that I sought opened up before my eyes. This is truly a case where the whole is greater than the sum of the parts. This insight came to me through my search in a fashion that simultaneously blindsided me and energized me. I hope you are encouraged by it as well.

An Arrival Foretold

> But you, Bethlehem Ephrathah, though you are small among the clans of Judah, out of you will come for me one who will be ruler over Israel, whose origins are from of old, from ancient times. (Micah 5:2)

> The scepter will not depart from Judah,
> nor the ruler's staff from between his
> feet, until he comes to whom it belongs
> and the obedience of the nations is his.
> (Genesis 49:10)

> Rejoice greatly, O Daughter of Zion!
> Shout, Daughter of Jerusalem! See, your
> king comes to you, righteous and having
> salvation, gentle and riding on a donkey, on
> a colt, the foal of a donkey. (Zechariah 9:9)

So what is so special about this Jesus? Why did my search determine that he stands out from any other character history presents to us? Why did he end up as one who may provide us with the proof we're seeking about God? We'll review a number of reasons, but one stands out immediately as truly significant.

....

**Jesus appeared upon the scene
as one who was announced.**

....

While most men simply arrive upon this planet, Jesus appeared upon the scene as one who was announced— one whose coming was foretold and anticipated centuries before. You see, more than three hundred prophecies existed about a coming Jewish Messiah. This expected Savior, or Deliverer, was to display attributes that showed he was anointed by God. In fact, the prophecies record that he was to be born a Jew, a descendant of David, of the tribe of Judah, and that he was to be sent from God to the whole world. Jesus Christ fulfilled every one of these prophecies.

Some of these three hundred-plus prophecies were written at least three centuries before Christ's birth, and most were written years before that. These prophecies about this one sent of God include details about the following:

- When he would be born (Daniel 9:24–25)
- What town he would be born in (Micah 5:2)
- What tribe he would be born in (Genesis 49:10)
- Who his specific ancestors were, by name (Genesis 21:12, 22:18, Jeremiah 23:5)
- That he would be called out of Egypt (Hosea 11:1)
- That the children of Bethlehem would be slain (Jeremiah 31:15)
- How he would die (Psalm 22:16, Isaiah 53:7, Micah 5:1, et. al)
- Who would accept him (Isaiah 60:3)
- Who would reject him (Isaiah 53:3, Psalm 69:8, 4)
- That he would be announced by *a voice crying in the wilderness* (Isaiah 40:3, Malachi 3:1)
- What miracles he would perform (Isaiah 35:5–6)

The details of these prophecies even get as specific as stating that he would be betrayed by one close to him for thirty pieces of silver and that the betrayer would throw the thirty pieces of silver into a field owned by a potter. They further state that he would suffer horribly when he died but that none of his bones would be broken. Also, when he was dying, he would be given a mixture of gall and vinegar to drink, and lots would be cast for his garments.

So what is the possibility that this is all chance—that someone fulfilled the prophecies who wasn't actually the one sent by God? Mathematicians have calculated that the probability of any one person fulfilling just eight of these prophecies is 1 in 10^{17}. Another way of writing this is 1 in 100,000,000,000,000,000.[13]

For Jesus Christ to have fulfilled just eight of the Messianic prophecies would have been a near impossibility, but consider this—throughout his lifetime, Christ fulfilled every one of the prophecies, the only exception being those that are written for a time still coming in the future.

If we are seeking evidence or proof of the existence of a God, it seems to me Christ's fulfillment of the Messianic prophecies should be enough to firmly grab our attention. But this marks only the beginning of what I uncovered …

---

[13] Peter W. Stoner, *Science Speaks* (Chicago: Moody Press, 1963), 100–07.

CHAPTER 6

The Bible

One important question to ask in this search for answers is if it is possible to maintain objectivity when referencing the Christian Bible. After all, don't Christians refer to the Bible as the *Word of God*?

The purpose of this book, at least at this juncture, is not to try to determine if the Bible is the Word of God. We're still at the point of gathering and sifting through evidence to establish if a God even exists. We will need to refer to the Bible, though, as it is the primary historical record of the life of Jesus of Nazareth. The reliability of the Bible as a document of historical value can be found in the fact that it is supported by many thousands of original manuscripts and manuscript fragments. In addition, the science of archaeology has unearthed plenty of evidence that confirms the legitimacy of the Bible record.

There are more sure marks of authenticity
in the Bible than in any profane history."

—attributed to Sir Isaac Newton
(1642–1727)

It's understandable that some will still question the validity of several of the stories chronicled about Jesus, due to their nature. These stories include accounts of supernatural occurrences that are not a part of most people's day-to-day experience. Couldn't his followers have made some of these stories up? Is it possible that they could have made all of it up? While either of these scenarios is possible, I researched a little further and found they're both highly unlikely for a couple of reasons.

The first reason to consider is that confirming information about Jesus Christ was recorded by others who were not associated with him. Cornelius Tacitus and Flavius Josephus, Roman and Jewish historians respectively, both made mention of Jesus Christ in their chronicles.[14] While initially one might consider this to be insignificant, I found that historians of that era typically only recorded accounts about great military leaders, political leaders, and noteworthy events.

The fact that these historians included information about Christ in their writings lends considerable credence to the other writings about Christ. They would have had no reason to include him in their accounts if he had not been an important figure. In fact, they probably never would have even heard of him if he hadn't had a significant historical impact. It was never their practice to record anything about any of the numerous religious nutcases running around at the time. In addition, neither of these historians had any vested interest in supporting the teachings of Jesus Christ through their writings.

---

[14]   Tacitus, *Annals* 15.44; Josephus, *Antiquities of the Jews* 18.3.3, 20.9.1.

The second reason it's improbable that the biblical account of Jesus was fabricated by his followers is that no contemporaries of Christ wrote anything to dispute the validity of the gospel record (the biblical books of Matthew, Mark, Luke, and John, which documented the details of Jesus' life) or of other popular texts about Christ circulating at the time. If anyone had written anything, it would have been the Jewish Pharisees and Sadducees. These were learned men who held the equivalent of doctorate degrees in the ancient world. They had every reason, and every resource, to write a record that denounced Christ, as his teachings strove to unravel much of what these academicians stood for.

So What about Them?

The Pharisees and the Sadducees were fully capable of writing accounts to refute the gospels, and they had ample motive to do so, yet they did not do it. Why is that? I believe it's because so many people knew the truth about Jesus, having witnessed his miracles firsthand, that writing any such documents would have discredited these established religious figures. Remember, much of what Jesus Christ did was in public settings in front of crowds of people. Also, the accounts we have give us only a sampling of the scope of Jesus' ministry. One revealing comment I read was made by the apostle John. He wrote, "Jesus did many other things as well. If every one of them were written down, I suppose that even the whole world would not have room for the books that would be written" (John 21:25).

> Jesus went throughout Galilee, teaching in their synagogues, preaching the good news of the kingdom, and healing every disease and sickness among the people. News about him spread all over Syria, and people brought to him all who were ill with various diseases, those suffering severe pain, the demon-possessed, those having seizures, and the paralyzed, and he healed them. Large crowds from Galilee, the Decapolis, Jerusalem, Judea and the region across the Jordan followed him. (Matthew 4:23–25)

> Some time after this, Jesus crossed to the far shore of the Sea of Galilee (that is, the Sea of Tiberias), and a great crowd of people followed him because they saw the miraculous signs he had performed on the sick. (John 6:1–2)

In short, far too many people witnessed the works of Christ firsthand for anyone to write anything that tried to deny those works and be taken seriously. A modern-day equivalent would be if I wrote that World War II never occurred. Too many people were directly involved in or impacted by this war for anyone to ever be able to deny it happened. If I tried, I would be laughed out of town.

A friend of mine asked me if it's possible that the Pharisees and Sadducees actually did write commentary to counter the stories about Christ found in the biblical record but the early Christian church tracked down and destroyed those documents.

While nearly anything is possible, the research I did showed me this scenario doesn't appear probable either. The Gnostic movement was an early response to the teachings of Jesus. Members of this movement wrote and circulated a number of manuscripts that contained teachings that leaders of the early Christian church considered cultish and contrary to what Jesus taught. Despite these views, the church members did not destroy these Gnostic writings. These writings, now known as the Gnostic gospels, are still around today.

The early Christian church did not destroy the Gnostic documents. Their strategy, instead, was to write their own responses to them (Galatians 2:8, 18, 1 Timothy 1:3-7, etc). For this reason, it seems highly unlikely that members of the early Christian church would have rounded up and destroyed anything the Pharisees and Sadducees would have written.

....

The Bible can be considered as historically valid a document as any other historical document we rely on.

....

I find it's impossible to have any kind of discussion about Jesus Christ without making some reference to the Bible narrative, as that book is where the majority of the historical account about Christ is found. For this reason, the next several pages will contain a number of references to biblical passages. The Bible can be considered as historically valid a document as any other historical document we rely on for information. Far more ancient documentation exists to support the biblical narrative about Jesus Christ than exists to support the account about Julius Caesar, for instance. If you have interest in researching this topic about the reliability of the Bible further, I recommend you take a look at a couple of books I have found helpful: *The Case for Christ* by Lee Strobel, and *The New Testament Documents: are they Reliable* by F.F. Bruce. These provide an intellectually sound approach to the subject, along with the latest research findings.

CHAPTER 7

Supernatural Activity

As already mentioned, Jesus Christ fulfilled every possible ancient prophecy about an individual who would be sent to man by God—yet there is much more to the story. You see, Christ was surrounded by supernatural events throughout his life. Unlike many other religious figures, whose professed supernatural interactions with God occurred in private, Jesus Christ's were witnessed by large crowds of people. These occurrences involved not only miracles performed by Christ but also episodes that occurred at the time of his birth, at his baptism, at his death, and after his death, as well.

The Birth of Christ

While a number of supernatural events occurred in conjunction with Christ's birth, several of these can be considered personal in nature. As a result, they did not leave behind enough witnesses for the purposes of this book. Some of these proceedings include the birth of Christ to a virgin, the special star that marked the location of his birth, the magi traveling from the east solely for the purpose of visiting him, the angel meeting with Mary about him, the angel meeting with Joseph about him, and the great company of angels appearing to shepherds concerning the birth of the promised Messiah from God.

Though these events surround the birth of Jesus Christ, they can lead the sincere seeker to questions of their validity because so few people were involved with them. This is not to say these events didn't occur; it is simply to state that they do not provide the types of examples I was seeking for this book. Only Mary and Joseph really know if Mary was a virgin when Jesus was conceived. For argument's sake, only Mary really knows for sure. It may be true that Mary was indeed a virgin. In fact, I believe she was. But there are not enough sources to confirm it for the purposes of this book. When looking at events for proof of something, we should keep our focus on only the events that involve enough witnesses to lend them practically unquestionable credence.

One historical event of a significant magnitude did occur at Christ's birth, though, that compels me to consider that his birth was special. When King Herod the Great heard of Jesus' birth, he issued a decree ordering that all male children under the age of two years who were born in Bethlehem and its surrounding towns be killed. It was Herod's hope that this move would kill Christ, for Herod had heard some of the prophecies we listed previously. He feared that Jesus was the fulfillment of them and that he would become a threat to Herod's throne. For a king as great and securely embedded in his position as Herod to make a move as drastic as this, it seems one has to respect the fact that the birth of this child holds some significance.

A Heavenly Proclamation

Through the centuries many people have been baptized, and Jesus Christ was no exception. At the beginning of his ministry, John the Baptist baptized Jesus in the Jordan River in the region of the desert of Judea. Even in this most common of religious practices, though, Jesus stands out from the rest of the crowd in extraordinary fashion.

Let's take note of the setting for this significant event in Christ's life: "And so John came, baptizing in the desert region and preaching a baptism of repentance for the forgiveness of sins. The whole Judean countryside and all the people of Jerusalem went out to him. Confessing their sins, they were baptized by him in the Jordan River" (Mark 1:4–5).

Here is an instance in which Christ was surrounded by crowds of people. At this point in his life, none of the people knew who he was. In their eyes, he was just like everyone else. As he approached John to be baptized, though, John the Baptist made an interesting statement in front of everyone:

> But John tried to deter him, saying, "I need to be baptized by you, and do you come to me?" Jesus replied, "Let it be so now; it is proper for us to do this to fulfill all righteousness." Then John consented. (Matthew 3:14–15)

John the Baptist, who had a ministry that was influential enough to cause many thousands of people to trek nearly twenty miles through the desert to find him, deferred his ministry to Jesus Christ as soon as he saw him. Some have argued that this holds no significance, though, as Jesus and John were cousins and could have set the whole scene up in advance. While this argument contains a degree of logic, I found the magnitude of the situation is confirmed by what follows:

> When all the people were being baptized, Jesus was baptized too. And as he was praying, heaven was opened and the Holy Spirit descended on him in bodily form like a dove. And a voice came from heaven: "You are my Son, whom I love; with you I am well pleased." (Luke 3:21–22)

How many other people throughout history, when they were baptized, caused heaven to open and a voice to speak concerning their significance? No one I can think of! And this happened in front of a multitude of people.

Remember, our search is for insight on whether a God exists, and if so, if he is involved in our lives. The event of Christ's baptism should certainly capture our attention; I know it did mine. Could it be that there is a God who is involved in our affairs? Could it be that at this event he tried to send us a message? While this event is certainly significant and highly compelling, I came to discover it is still only the beginning ...

Christ the Miracle Worker

Probably the most popular stories about the life of Jesus Christ involve the many miracles he performed. Accounts of these happenings are relayed in Sunday school classes and children's books around the world. I realized that because I had heard these stories so often, and starting at such a young age, I had neglected to consider their value when weighing spiritual matters in my later years. I can't help but believe this must be true for at least some others as well. In addition, enough "miracle workers" have emerged over the centuries to cause the concept of supernatural miracles to become almost commonplace.

Unfortunately, like with everything else, for every legitimate person who has performed a miracle, there is a fraud who causes the average seeker of truth to become disenchanted with the whole notion. This is unfortunate because if a God exists who wants to get our attention, one way he could do so is by displaying his power through supernatural miracles.

When I considered the miracles that Christ performed, I began to recognize a couple of facets that set his miracles apart from those of many others. First I became amazed at the wide variety of miracles Jesus performed beyond just the more-common healing type of miracle. He changed water into wine, multiplied the food of one person to feed thousands of people, walked on water, and calmed storms instantly, thus demonstrating his power over nature itself.

....

Most of Jesus' miracles were visible – they could be seen.

....

The second feature I discovered about the miracles of Jesus is that his miracles were usually visible. Causing lame people to walk and blind people to see, feeding multitudes of people, curing leprosy, and raising people from the dead are all miracles people can actually see. A concern of many seekers I've spoken with who want to know if miracles are legitimate is that a large number of the "miracles" that are produced today involve the healing of internal diseases and problems no one can really observe visually or follow up on to see if the "healing" remains permanent. They have no way of discerning which miracles are legitimate and which are not. The visible nature of Christ's miracles satisfies this reasonable concern. Finally—and I know I've said this before—many of Christ's miracles were witnessed by large numbers of people.

Because the miracles Jesus performed are so numerous, we won't delve into their details. Instead, to gain a perspective on the variety and types of miracles he performed, let us simply review a list of these supernatural events. It is recorded that Jesus did the following miracles:

- turned water into wine
- healed a man of leprosy
- healed the Roman centurion's servant without even seeing him

- brought a widow's son back to life from the dead
- healed Peter's mother-in-law
- calmed the violent storm on the Sea of Galilee
- cast demons out of two demon-possessed men who blocked a town road
- gave his disciples a large catch of fish
- healed a paralyzed man
- raised the daughter of Jairus, a synagogue ruler, from the dead
- healed a woman of a bleeding problem when she simply touched his cloak
- gave sight to two blind men
- healed a man who was mute and cast demons out of him
- restored the shriveled hand of a man to full function
- raised Lazarus from the dead
- gave sight and speech to a blind, mute man and cast demons out of him
- multiplied food to feed over five thousand people with five loaves of bread and two fish
- walked on water, over three miles across the Sea of Galilee
- Cast demons out of the daughter of a Canaanite woman
- Multiplied food to feed over four thousand people with seven loaves of bread and a few small fish
- cast a seizure-causing demon out of a young boy
- got a coin from a fish of the exact denomination needed
- gave sight to two more blind men

- made a fig tree wither
- healed a man who was deaf and mute
- cast a demon out of a man in a local synagogue
- healed another man who was blind
- healed a woman who had been crippled for eighteen years
- healed a man suffering from a fluid problem that affected parts of his body
- cured ten men with leprosy
- replaced the ear on the high priest's servant after it was cut off
- healed the dying son of a royal official without visiting him
- healed the man at the pool of Bethesda
- gave sight to a man who was born blind
- gave his disciples another large catch of fish

Though this list may appear exhaustive, I am reminded again of the final words of the apostle John in his gospel: "Jesus did many other things as well. If every one of them were written down, I suppose that even the whole world would not have room for the books that would be written" (John 21:25).

While listing the miracles of Christ has some value, I benefited from taking a moment to review the documented responses of the witnesses to these miracles. This exercise provided me with an additional perspective on these events. Here are some of the responses:

As am result, Jesus could no longer enter a town openly but stayed outside in lonely places. Yet the people still came to him from everywhere. (Mark 1:45)

Yet the news about him spread all the more, so that crowds of people came to hear him and to be healed of their sicknesses. (Luke 5:15)

Then the men who had been sent returned to the house and found the servant well. (Luke 7:10)

The men were amazed and asked, "What kind of man is this? Even the winds and the waves obey him!" (Matthew 8:27)

When those tending the pigs saw what had happened, they ran off and reported this in the town and countryside, and the people went out to see what had happened. When they came to Jesus, they found the man from whom the demons had gone out, sitting at Jesus' feet, dressed and in his right mind; and they were afraid. Those who had seen it told the people how the demon-possessed man had been cured. Then all the people of the region of the Gerasenes asked Jesus to leave them, because they were overcome with fear. So he got into the boat and left. (Luke 8:34–37)

The man from whom the demons had gone out begged to go with him, but Jesus sent him away, saying, "Return home and tell how much God has done for you." So the man went away and told all over town how much Jesus had done for him. (Luke 8:38–39)

Immediately he stood up in front of them, took what he had been lying on and went home praising God. Everyone was amazed and gave praise to God. They were filled with awe and said, "We have seen remarkable things today." (Luke 5:25–26)

They were all filled with awe and praised God. "A great prophet has appeared among us," they said. "God has come to help his people." This news about Jesus spread throughout Judea and the surrounding country. (Luke 7:16–17)

The crowd was amazed and said, "Nothing like this has ever been seen in Israel." (Matthew 9:33b)

But the Pharisees said, "It is by the prince of demons that he drives out demons." (Matthew 9:34)

And his hand was completely restored. Then the Pharisees went out and began to plot with the Herodians how they might kill Jesus. (Mark 3:5–6)

When the demon left, the man who had been mute spoke, and the crowd was amazed. But some of them said, "By Beelzebub, the prince of demons, he is driving out demons." (Luke 11:14–15)

When the disciples saw him walking on the lake, they were terrified. (Matthew 14:26)

Then those who were in the boat worshiped him, saying, "Truly you are the Son of God." (Matthew 14:33)

After the people saw the miraculous sign that Jesus did, they began to say, "Surely this is the Prophet who is to come into the world." (John 6:14)

Therefore many of the Jews who had come to visit Mary, and had seen what Jesus did, put their faith in him. (John 11:45)

And they were all amazed at the greatness of God. (Luke 9:43)

Immediately he received his sight and followed Jesus, praising God. When all the people saw it, they also praised God. (Luke 18:43)

People were overwhelmed with amazement. "He has done everything well," they said. "He even makes the deaf hear and the mute speak." (Mark 7:37)

The people were all so amazed that they asked each other, "What is this? A new teaching—and with authority! He even gives orders to evil spirits and they obey him." (Mark 1:27)

So he and all his household believed. (John 4:53)

Then the man said, "Lord, I believe," and he worshiped him. (John 9:38)

So they pulled their boats up on shore, left everything and followed him. (Luke 5:11)

The famous quote attributed to Abraham Lincoln states, "You can fool some of the people all of the time, and all of the people some of the time, but you cannot fool all of the people all of the time." Throughout the centuries, people have come and gone who have provided occasional miraculous signs and wonders. Some of these individuals are remembered by a few, but most are forgotten. The responses to Jesus' miracles, however, included amazement, awe, and wonder. Debates were sparked, crowds followed him everywhere, and entire towns sought him out for healing. Some hated him for rocking the established religious hierarchy and sought to kill him, while others left all they had and followed him. Some even worshiped him as God. These people could not have simply been fooled by parlor tricks; this was too big. They were challenged by a consistent display of miracles that were performed on their friends, their relatives, their neighbors, and even themselves.

....

**The miracles of Christ
truly set him apart
from any other individual
who has ever lived.**

....

All that Christ did was well known far and wide. The responses of the people to the works Jesus performed provide at least some degree of legitimacy to those works. As the quote says, "You cannot fool all of the people all of the time." It seems to me the miracles of Christ hold validity, are extra-human in nature, and truly set him apart from any other individual who has ever lived. But there is still more …

CHAPTER 8

Christ's Death

Similar to his birth, baptism, and life, Jesus Christ's death was surrounded by a number of supernatural events. I find these events add to the story of an individual who stands out as entirely different from any other person who has ever walked the face of the earth—and who potentially could provide us with some answers to our questions about the existence of God.

So what happened on the day of Christ's death that sets him apart from the rest of us? First, the gospels record that on the day of Christ's crucifixion upon a Roman cross, "From the sixth hour until the ninth hour darkness came over all the land" (Matthew 27:45). All of the research I found informs us that this period of time was from about noon to about 3:00 p.m.—an unusual time for darkness. Christ was crucified at about 9:00 a.m., and he died at about 3:00 p.m. (Mark 15:25–37). As soon as he died, the darkness left the land.

In addition to this strange darkness, some other supernatural events occurred at the exact moment Jesus died.

> And when Jesus had cried out again in a
> loud voice, he gave up his spirit. At that
> moment the curtain of the temple was
> torn in two from top to bottom. The earth
> shook and the rocks split. The tombs broke
> open and the bodies of many holy people
> who had died were raised to life ... When
> the centurion and those with him who
> were guarding Jesus saw the earthquake
> and all that had happened, they were
> terrified, and exclaimed, "Surely he was
> the Son of God!" (Matthew 27:50–52, 54)

Any of these events happening simultaneously with a person's death could be taken as coincidence; however, to have all of these occurrences happening at once should cause one to raise an intrigued eyebrow, at the least.

Understandably, some question these accounts detailing Christ's death due to an apprehension that the writers, who were followers of Christ, fabricated them in order to further a religious agenda they had developed. In essence, some people are concerned that the gospel writers were simply trying to sell them on a new religion based on Christ's teachings.

These concerns are legitimate and can't be dismissed lightly. As I pondered these thoughts, I kept returning to the lack of response from the Jewish Pharisees and Sadducees. Accounts of the events surrounding Christ's death circulated around the region where he lived, yet none of the intellectual challengers wrote anything to counter them, though they had the education and resources to be able to do so. Once again, it seems to me that they would have only discredited themselves by such an action, as a massive number of people personally witnessed the events and would have declared that the challengers should never be taken seriously again.

Alive Again?

As incredible as the collection of events surrounding Christ's death may seem, something happened afterward that should attract the attention of even the most wary person who is weighing evidence for proof about God. Regarding the "holy people" we just read about who were raised back to life, the apostle Matthew records in his account, "They came out of the tombs, and after Jesus' resurrection they went into the holy city and appeared to many people" (Matthew 27:53). These people went into Jerusalem when? After *Jesus' resurrection*.

....

Christ demonstrated power not only over death in other people but also over his own death.

....

Along with the other events surrounding Jesus' death, accounts exist of his resurrection occurring three days later. This is extraordinary as it would mean that Christ demonstrated power not only over death in other people but also over his own death. Previously he had even gone so far as to predict his own resurrection (Matthew

12:39–40, 16:21, John 2:18–22). In addition, he stated that he had the power to resurrect himself: "'I lay down my life—only to take it up again. No one takes it from me, but I lay it down of my own accord. I have authority to lay it down and authority to take it up again. This command I received from my Father'" (John 10:17–18). In all of my research, I could find no one else who ever lived who could make a claim of power over death like this—and fulfill it!

The record of Jesus' appearances following his death includes revealing himself to a woman named Mary Magdalene and another woman also named Mary at his empty tomb. He then revealed himself to Mary Magdalene in a garden, then to two people traveling on the road to Emmaus, then to his disciple Peter, then to ten of his disciples who were together in the upper room of a house in Jerusalem, then to seven disciples who were fishing on the Sea of Galilee, then to eleven disciples on a mountain, then to more than five hundred men at once, then to his disciple James, then to his disciples at his ascension, and then eventually to Paul the apostle. When some doubted he was actually physically alive, he had Thomas and the other disciples touch his wounds. He also ate a piece of broiled fish in front of them. The women at the tomb knelt before him and held his feet, and he cooked and ate breakfast with his disciples on another occasion.

I learned that some of the primary arguments made by skeptics of the accounts of Jesus' resurrection included the notions that he never actually died in the first place, that his disciples fabricated the whole resurrection story, that the disciples were confused, and that the disciples/apostles were not actually the ones who recorded the gospel record but that it was recorded by someone much later.

Plenty has been written both for and against these arguments, so we will not delve into these debates further. However, I feel it's significant to note something else I found that relates to this. Historical tradition and early church documents indicate that Jesus' disciples died painful deaths as martyrs, refusing to deny what Christ did.

His Disciples

So what about the testimony of Christ's disciples? While it's possible for one or two individuals to decide to die a martyr's death instead of admitting to creating a fabrication, I submit that it is not possible for an entire group of twelve men (counting the apostle Paul, who received a personal visit from the resurrected Christ) to endure a lifetime of beatings, imprisonment, persecution, and suffering, capped by a torturous death, simply to propagate a lie. In fact, I don't believe they would do this if they had even the slightest inclination that what they stood for was anything less than absolute truth.

Let's think about it for a moment. These men suffered, their families most likely suffered, they didn't profit from their testimony or actions, and their mission involved a great amount of effort and personal sacrifice. No one in his right mind would endure this for a lie! And no—not all twelve of them were out of their right minds.

One young woman I have spoken with stated that this commitment to death by Christ's followers was no different than the mass suicide actions of any cult group we have heard about on the news over the past few years. I had to tell her that I see the devotion of Christ's followers as different.

I find the actions of these individuals to be different for several reasons. First, during the period when they suffered and died, their leader was gone. Cult groups generally require the presence of a strong leader to keep them brainwashed into committing an act as extreme as suicide, but Christ had died and left already. Second, Christ's followers were beaten and tortured, starved, stoned by angry mobs, jailed, and shipwrecked over a lifetime. Their suffering didn't last momentarily. It required great endurance—the kind of endurance that a lie could never produce.

Finally, Christ's followers were not a close-knit group. They argued about favoring Jews over Gentiles (Galatians 2:11), they fought over who should be seated next to Christ in his kingdom (Matthew 20:20–24), they disputed about which one of them was the greatest (Luke 22:24), and they disagreed to the point of permanent separation over who should accompany them on a journey (Acts 15:36–40).

....

They found Jesus to be the real thing, not a fake, and they felt whatever he taught and stood for was worth the sacrifice and devotion of an entire lifetime.

....

No cult mentality existed; Jesus' disciples were not unified, and they were not even physically in the same location when they suffered and eventually died. They did so separately and frequently alone, yet they remained devoted to Christ and what he taught. By all accounts, it appears they found Jesus to be the real thing, not a fake, and they felt whatever he taught and stood for was worth the sacrifice and devotion of an entire lifetime.

Another friend of mine asked me how the actions of Christ's followers are any different from other religious zealots who surrender their lives in suicide bombings. My view remains that these are different situations. First, suicide bombers frequently have strong leadership encouraging them. Second, it is not a lifetime of suffering they endure but an instant. And finally, they are not receiving the suffering upon themselves but are instead inflicting it on others.

Like No Other

Based on the incredible amount of supernatural activity that surrounded the death of Jesus Christ; the unwavering devotion of his followers through suffering and even death for testifying that he died and three days later rose again to life; and the number of people besides the disciples who witnessed these events, it seems that not only is the crucifixion/resurrection account valid but that Jesus Christ is truly an extraordinary individual who is worthy of our attention. No other person or even event in history comes close to showing us the magnitude of spiritual power that was both displayed by him and that followed him throughout the entirety of his lifetime.

To top it all off, when it was time to go, Jesus didn't even leave this earth in regular fashion.

> After he said this, he was taken up before their very eyes, and a cloud hid him from their sight. They were looking intently up into the sky as he was going, when suddenly two men dressed in white stood beside them. "Men of Galilee," they said, "why do you stand here looking into the sky? This same Jesus, who has been taken from you into heaven, will come back in the same way you have seen him go into heaven." (Acts 1:9–11)

One final thought: after Christ left this earth, his followers went on to live their lives fully devoted to his teachings, even to the point of suffering and dying painful deaths, as already mentioned. Their testimony did not consist simply of words, however. The expression of their testimony was backed by a demonstration of the same supernatural power Christ displayed during his time on earth. I found this to be far from coincidence, giving us yet one more nugget to consider regarding the life of this remarkable individual.

So what does this all mean? Could Jesus Christ be the contact with the supreme, omnipotent Being that we seek? Or could he be someone else altogether? As I examined this further, I found the account of this man becomes even more extraordinary.

CHAPTER 9

The Words of a Miracle Worker

To summarize my search for answers about God, I learned that the disciplines of science and philosophy have fallen short in their ability to either reveal or determine concrete truth on the subject. In addition, I found a look into the realm of religion and religious figures has curiously left us empty-handed—with the exception of one man.

This man, Jesus Christ, drew attention at his birth, had heaven open at his baptism, and was identified as "Son" by a voice that spoke from heaven. He healed the sick, made the lame walk, gave sight to the blind, raised people from the dead, and controlled the forces of nature.

This man was loved by the people, hated by the established religious hierarchy, and followed by many. His death was surrounded by the same degree of supernatural activity that accompanied his life. He even told his followers he would raise himself from the dead, and he did just that! Just in case any would doubt that he was alive again, he appeared to over five hundred people, many of them gathered together (1 Corinthians 15:3–8).

All that Christ did was witnessed by hundreds of thousands of people over his lifetime. Because of this, no one could build any kind of legitimate-sounding case to try to refute the gospel records that recorded his life. His disciples refused to disavow allegiance to him, following him and his teachings to their own suffering and deaths. In addition, they demonstrated much of the same extraordinary power that he did during his existence on earth.

When Jesus finally departed the earth, he did so by physically rising upward through the clouds into a place referred to as heaven, again in front of a sizeable gathering of people. As if all this were not enough, the specifics of his birth, the events of his life, particulars about his person, and the details of his death were all foretold centuries before by Hebrew prophets who stated that these signs would follow the one who was to be sent by God to bring salvation and freedom to his people Israel and eventually to all mankind.

What Did He Say?

No other individual has ever existed who demonstrated the kind of power that Jesus Christ did. No other individual has ever been surrounded by the degree of supernatural activity that followed Jesus throughout his entire time on earth. No other leader has been able to pass on power to his followers in the manner that Jesus did, and no other person has ever had his life and purpose so accurately prophesied about centuries before in the manner that Jesus did. Because of this, I took a closer look at what Jesus said in order to determine if he can lead us to the answers we seek. It seems to me the words of a man of this caliber are more than worthy of our consideration.

About Himself

> The woman said, "I know that Messiah" (called Christ) "is coming. When he comes, he will explain everything to us." Then Jesus declared, "I who speak to you am he." (John 4:25–26)

> Then Jesus declared, "I am the bread of life. He who comes to me will never go hungry, and he who believes in me will never be thirsty." (John 6:35)

> For I have come down from heaven not to do my will but to do the will of him who sent me. (John 6:38)

> I am the living bread that came down from heaven. (John 6:51)

> Jesus answered, "My teaching is not my own. It comes from him who sent me.'" (John 7:16)

> But he continued, "You are from below; I am from above. You are of this world; I am not of this world. I told you that

you would die in your sins; if you do not believe that I am the one I claim to be, you will indeed die in your sins." (John 8:23–24)

I came from God and now am here. I have not come on my own; but he sent me. (John 8:42)

"I tell you the truth," Jesus answered, "before Abraham was born, I am!" (John 8:58)

"Do you believe in the Son of Man?" "Who is he, sir?" the man asked. "Tell me so that I may believe in him." Jesus said, "You have now seen him; in fact, he is the one speaking with you." (John 9:35–37)

"I and the Father are one." (John 10:30)

"Anyone who has seen me has seen the Father." (John 14:9)

Simon Peter answered, "You are the Christ, the Son of the living God." Jesus replied, "Blessed are you, Simon son of Jonah, for this was not revealed to you by man, but by my Father in heaven." (Matthew 16:16–17)

> They all asked, "Are you then the Son
> of God?" He replied, "You are right in
> saying I am." (Luke 22:70)

One theme that stood out to me as I reviewed the words of this remarkable man is that throughout his life, Jesus Christ repeatedly referred to his *Father* as being *God*. He also frequently interchanged the two words—*Father* and *God*—in statements he made. Jesus stated many times that he and the Father are one, and he made multiple mentions of a spirit—the Holy Spirit—as being in union with himself and his Father (e.g., John 15:26, Matthew 10:20).

Jesus referred to his Father, himself, and the Holy Spirit as being on equal footing (e.g., Matthew 28:19); thus he reinforced the doctrine of a triune God or a God who is the perfect union of three distinct individual beings. In essence, Jesus told us that *there is a God* and *exactly who that God is!*

Just to make sure we didn't miss his message, Jesus made reference to the nature of God and to his own nature on multiple occasions. It is recorded in Scripture that Jesus stated the following things:

- at least twelve times that he came from heaven (John 6:38, 6:51, etc.)
- at least seventeen times that he was the Son of God (Matthew 16:16–17, John 10:36, etc.)
- at least two times that he was the promised Messiah (John 4:25–26, Matthew 16:16–17)

- at least fourteen times that he was the provider of true eternal life (John 6:35, 6:40, etc.)
- at least eleven times that he was sent by God (John 7:16, 8:42, etc.)
- at least five times that he was God (John 8:58, 10:30–33, 14:9, Revelation 1:8, 22:13)

Vernon C. Grounds, in *The Reason for Our Hope,* ascribes the following quote to Napoleon:

> I know men; and I tell you that Jesus Christ is not a man. Superficial minds see a resemblance between Christ and the founders of empires, and the gods of other religions. That resemblance does not exist. There is between Christianity and whatever other religions the distance of infinity ... Everything in Christ astonishes me. His spirit overawes me, and His will confounds me. Between Him and whoever else in the world, there is no possible term of comparison. He is truly a being by Himself. His ideas and sentiments, the truth which He announces, His manner of convincing, are not explained either by human organization or by the nature of things ... The nearer I approach, the more carefully I examine, everything is above me—everything remains grand, of a grandeur which overpowers. His religion is a revelation from an intelligence which

certainly is not that of man … One can absolutely find nowhere, but in Him alone, the imitation or the example of His life … I search in vain in history to find the similar to Jesus Christ, or anything which can approach the gospel. Neither history, nor humanity, nor the ages, nor nature, offer me anything with which I am able to compare it or to explain it. Here everything is extraordinary.[15]

Friends, from what I can see, our search for evidence of a God is over. Jesus Christ has shown us that we are created beings living on a created planet that is spinning through a created universe. The apostle John puts it like this when he refers to Jesus as the very Word of God who spoke our world into being:

"In the beginning was the Word, and the Word was with God, and the Word was God. He was with God in the beginning. Through him all things were made; without him nothing was made that has been made. In him was life, and that life was the light of men. The light shines in the darkness, but the darkness has not understood it.

---

[15] Vernon C. Grounds, *The Reason for Our Hope* (Chicago: Moody Press, 1945).

There came a man who was sent from God; his name was John. He came as a witness to testify concerning that light, so that through him all men might believe. He himself was not the light; he came only as a witness to the light. The true light that gives light to every man was coming into the world."

(John 1:1–9)

There is a God, and he does care about us, as he has chosen to reveal himself to us through the person of Jesus Christ. Jesus is the observable proof that science searches for concerning the existence of a Creator. He is the God that religion seeks and the answer to the questions of philosophy.

....

Christ told us exactly who God is, and stated that he, himself, is a part of this triune being.

....

Christ told us exactly who God is, and stated that he, himself, is a part of this triune being. He then provided mankind with all the evidence necessary to demonstrate who he was and to substantiate all of the claims that he made. No other figure in history ever demonstrated the power to back up his words in the manner that Jesus

Christ did. God has sent us a message about himself, and he has sent it loud and clear!

What Else Did He Say?

While Jesus Christ has demonstrated more than sufficiently who God is, could it be that other deities exist besides him? After all, there are many other religions and individual beliefs in the world that point people to other gods. Perhaps Christ simply told us about himself, his Father, and the Holy Spirit but didn't feel obligated to tell us that there are other gods out there—perhaps leaving it up to those other deities and their followers to do that themselves. On a related note, if Christ did actually reveal to us the only God that exists, then could it be that the many religions of the world are in place to provide multiple avenues to him?

As stated already, it would be impossible for the ideas of the multiple religions of the world to coexist logically because they are ideologically opposed to each other. While this makes sense, let's consider what Jesus had to say on the matter. It seems to me he is the only one, to date, to present any qualifications to speak about it.

Concerning the issue of the existence of multiple gods, Jesus quickly puts the matter to rest.

> My Father, who has given them to me, is greater than all. (John 10:29)

> I praise you, Father, Lord of heaven and earth. (Matthew 11:25)

I am the Alpha and the Omega, the First and the Last, the Beginning and the End. (Revelation 22:13)

Then Jesus came to them and said, "All authority in heaven and on earth has been given to me." (Matthew 28:18)

Again the high priest asked him, "Are you the Christ, the Son of the Blessed One?" "I am," said Jesus. "And you will see the Son of Man sitting at the right hand of the Mighty One and coming on the clouds of heaven." (Mark 14:61–62)

"I am returning to my Father and your Father, to my God and your God." (John 20:17)

In addition to making these statements, Jesus never refers to his Father as *a* god, *this* god, *one of the gods*, or any other verbiage that would lead us to think that he is anything other than *the only* God. In fact, Jesus refers to him as "*the only true God*" (John 17:3).

Concerning the existence of multiple pathways to God, Jesus said, "I am the way and the truth and the life. No one comes to the Father except through me" (John 14:6). The one who definitively revealed God to us—the only one in history to do so—stated that there is no other way to God except through him. This would mean that according to Jesus, no religion that states that Jesus is simply a "great prophet"; no faith that states that humans are capable of becoming gods; or any belief system that fails to acknowledge Jesus Christ as the only way, the truth, and the life can be right.

Friends, this perspective on Christ, on other religious figures, and on the gods promoted by the world's many religions will lead some of you to rejoice that you have finally found clarity in this confusing matter. You will be inspired by Christ to accept the knowledge that there is a God, and you will want to learn more about who he is. For others of you, though, this perspective will be a hard concept to accept, as it may fly in the face of everything you've been told and everything you have understood up to this point in your lives. Some may even feel anger regarding this.

The purpose of this book was never to create dismay or anger. It is to share the findings I made in my own personal journey to find proof of God. You may recall one of the premises I stated at the beginning of this book— that if a God exists out there who desires a relationship with us, he will reveal himself to us in a very clear, very specific way. In other words, this God will make sure we know, without a doubt, who he is. I found that a God does exist and that he has revealed himself in this manner, by walking among us in the person of Jesus Christ.

....

**God wants us to walk in faith,
but he never asked us to
walk in *blind* faith.**

....

Some people have asked me, *"But what about faith—why seek proof?"* I have no problem with living by faith in God. I do it every day, as he has not revealed the future to us. I have discovered through the years that he wants us to trust him for all circumstances in our lives. He also wants us to trust him that he is who he says he is. He wants us to walk in faith, trusting him—but I don't recall that he ever asked us to walk in *blind* faith. God revealed himself clearly enough to us that we could trust him, that we could know who he is, and that we could have a real relationship with him.

Based on what Christ taught, it becomes clear that God never intended for us to spend our lives struggling to find him based on feelings, impressions, or even personal experiences. These kinds of events are vague. They can lead us to a wide variety of ideas about who God is. This is also true of the teachings of many of the major religions of the world. Their doctrines conflict and lead us to confusion. The founders and leaders of these religions share that they have received visions from God, heard his voice directly, were visited by an angel, or received scrolls or golden plaques with God's words on them. As mentioned previously, the scrolls disappeared, the golden plaques evaporated, the angels and visions were never seen by others, and the voice of God was never overheard by anyone else.

I have found it interesting that most of the time when I ask Christians—followers of Christ—why they believe in God, their answers would fall into the "personal" category. "I know there's a God because he lives in my heart," or "I know he's there because of what he's done in my life" are typical responses I would receive. Never have I heard, "Because two thousand years ago God came to earth and showed us who he is."

Jesus Christ broke the mold among those who have sought to reveal God to us. He was different from all of the others. He was public, he was available, he was obtuse, and he displayed power never seen before or since. He was and still is God. When I consider what Christ did and what he said, I come to the realization that we have a God who knows each of us personally. I also discover that he wants to be known personally by each of us.

....

**Why do I believe what I do, and
how does that measure up
against what Jesus Christ has shown me?**

....

Once more, the intent of this book was never to ostracize or irritate anyone. It was simply to challenge each of us to ask *why*. *Why do I believe what I do, and how does that measure up against what Jesus Christ has shown me?* Then each person can make an informed decision about how he or she wants to live. As for me, though, I find myself convinced that Christ has shown us the God we have sought and the God we need in our lives.

CHAPTER 10

What Does This Mean for Me?

All that I've learned about Jesus Christ has convinced me more than ever that he is who he says he is—the son of the Living God. He, his Father, and the Holy Spirit together form the being we know as God.

Someone once told me to think of God like an egg. An egg is comprised of the yoke, the white, and the shell. Each component has a different purpose and function, but together they're known simply as an egg. If any component is missing, the egg ceases to be an egg any longer. The Father, the Son, and the Holy Spirit have different purposes and functions, but each is as important as the other.

Okay, so if Jesus has answered the question about the existence of God for us and has given himself as that answer, what does that have to do with me? I've been asked this question on a number of occasions, and I've found the best approach to the answer is actually to ask another question. *Why did Jesus suffer and die on the Roman crucifix? That seems so ungodlike.*

The Need for a Savior

When Jesus found himself hanging on the cross on that fateful day so long ago, he was not in unexpected circumstances. God had not been captured by his creation. On the contrary, Christ had told his disciples several times that he would die in this manner, well in advance of the event (John 3:14, 8:28, 10:14–18, 12:33–34, etc.).

> Now as Jesus was going up to Jerusalem, he took the twelve disciples aside and said to them, "We are going up to Jerusalem, and the Son of Man will be betrayed to the chief priests and the teachers of the law. They will condemn him to death and will turn him over to the Gentiles to be mocked and flogged and crucified. On the third day he will be raised to life!" (Matthew 20:17–19)

Jesus wasn't caught off guard when he was crucified, as just the opposite had occurred. *He planned it.*

But why would God do such a thing? Why would he come to earth to reveal himself to us and then die a human death? From our perspective this doesn't make any sense. From his perspective, though, Christ knew exactly what he was doing and why. To put it simply, he did it for us. He did it for you and for me. He did it to set us free.

....

**Sin is at the root of all that
holds us hostage.**

....

Free? Free from what? Many of us feel that we have freedom already. We can make choices, we can direct the course of our lives, or we can live how we want. Jesus said he came to free us from something bigger, though. Jesus revealed throughout his ministry that he came to set us free from everything that entraps or enslaves us in this life. He wants to free us from things like worry or want, despair, addiction, or even the restricting feelings of insignificance or purposelessness we can experience. There is one problem that plagues mankind more than any other, though, and that was his primary target. That problem is called sin. Jesus made it clear that sin is at the root of all that holds us hostage.

The Sin Problem

In Romans 3:23 we read, "For all have sinned and fall short of the glory of God." Before we can understand why Jesus came to earth and performed the acts he did and spoke the words he spoke, we need to understand our condition. We need to understand the situation every one of us is in.

When I read this passage in the book of Romans, it tells me that every person who ever lived on this planet—whether two thousand years ago or today; whether in Asia, Europe, or South America; no matter what race, religion, or culture; and no matter whether male or female—every one of us ("*all*") have sinned. So what is this sin? Many scholars understand the original Greek word for sin used in this passage to be an archery term that simply means to "miss the mark."

Missing a mark doesn't sound very significant, so we need to be careful not to under-define what our sin is, as the cost of our sin is very high. It is not simply breaking some rules that God gave us (Deuteronomy 5:7–21), though that's part of it. It's not just that we have a sinful nature (Romans 5:12–14), though that is part of it too. It's not even that we've rejected our Creator's rightful place of authority in our life (Colossians 1:16). It's all of that together and then some. We have fallen *short of the glory of God*. In God's eyes, we are not the beings he originally made in his image (Genesis 1:27). We are now different. We have fallen.

Some of us may feel we've come close to hitting the mark, while others know that they missed not only the mark but the entire target completely. Regardless, we're all in the same boat. We have all fallen short of the standard God set up for us, and we are not the people he created us to be.

The Wages of Sin

One thing we must consider about sin is that we need to avoid the temptation of finger-pointing. I cannot say you're a worse sinner than I am, and neither can you tell someone else that they're worse than you. We can't conclude that we're okay because others' sins appear more corrupt or evil than ours. Romans 6:23 clarifies why we can't do this, as it says, "For the wages of sin is death" (Romans 6:23a). This passage tells us that we all receive the same penalty—death.

In the eyes of our Creator, sin is sin, and it all earns the same consequence. We may see our shortcomings and those of others as ranging from mild to severe, but that doesn't matter from the perspective of the Eternal. He sees that none of us are conducting our lives as he intended. None of us meets his standard. Our disease runs far deeper than just the actions we can see with our human eyes.

> People will be lovers of themselves, lovers of money, boastful, proud, abusive, disobedient to their parents, ungrateful, unholy, without love, unforgiving, slanderous, without self-control, brutal, not lovers of the good, treacherous, rash, conceited, lovers of pleasure rather than lovers of God—having a form of godliness but denying its power. (2 Timothy 3:2–5)

> We all, like sheep, have gone astray, each of us has turned to his own way. (Isaiah 53:6)

So what, then, is this *death* that is mentioned in the Romans passage? Taking a closer look reveals that the word *death* is both eternal and temporal—both for the future and for the present.

We all understand the kinds of problems we face on a daily basis as humans. Our jealousies, selfishness, pride, anxieties, and failure to give our Creator his due place in our lives ("sin" according to Jesus' standards) lead to broken relationships, depression, abuse, fights, cheating, stealing, and even murder and war. Instead of building others up, we criticize them and cut them down. We self-seekingly make plans for our lives with little thought of the plans God may have for us. We then try to cover up our sin by justifying or even spiritualizing our decisions. Look at the mess we've made of his world! This is opposite of the good life God intended us to have (Genesis 1:31, John 10:10). It is the form of death we deal with in our time on this planet.

An Eternal Price

Jesus also mentioned the other side—the eternal side of this death—on numerous occasions when he referred to a place he called hell. Studying the various statements Jesus made about hell reveals that it is a place of eternal solitude, regret, suffering, and torture (Luke 16:19–31). He referred to it as a place of eternal punishment (Matthew 25:46) and a "fiery furnace, where there will be weeping and gnashing of teeth" (Matthew 13:42).

**Jesus never used hell as a
threat with people.**

I found it interesting to note, as I read Jesus' comments about hell, that he never used hell as a threat with people. Sure, there were a couple of occasions where he mentioned hell while blasting a religious leader or two, but Jesus' references to hell were more a statement of facts—not threats. Jesus didn't tell people, "Follow me or you're going to hell." Jesus knew that due to our fallen condition, we were already headed there. It's like the Romans passage says: "For the wages of sin is death" (Romans 6:23a).

Some people ask how a loving God can send people to a place like hell. But Jesus' emphasis throughout his ministry was to set people free from this consequence. Because of our sinful natures, we are already destined for hell. The Bible is clear that hell was not made for man but was actually created for the devil and his angels—beings who rejected the Creator (Matthew 25:41). By doing the same, we walk away from God, along with his protections and blessings, and we knowingly or unknowingly join with those beings who are encamped against him.

My search through the Bible finds no reference to our Creator taking pleasure in our demise. In fact, just the opposite occurred. Jesus actually wept over our inability to see what we're doing to ourselves (Luke 19:41–42). God does not send anyone to hell; instead, he is actively trying to rescue us (1 Timothy 2:3–4). He wants to free us from all of the holds that sin has on our lives—both currently and for eternity.

So, all of us have a problem—it's called sin. We, as sinful beings, never reach the potential our Creator intended for us. Our sinfulness doesn't just describe what we do; it defines who we are. Instead of being the children of a perfect and holy God, we are now objects of his wrath (Ephesians 2:3). We miss out on the perfect, eternal union our Creator desires to have with us, and instead we face an eternity in hell.

Sin is our problem. Adam introduced sin to the human race (Genesis 3, Romans 5:12), and we keep it active in our lives and in the world today. There is hope for our condition, though, and it's provided to us by our God who gives both grace and mercy!

God of Love

The first half of Romans 6:23 reads, "For the wages of sin is death," but this is not the end of the story. This verse finishes with, "But the gift of God is eternal life in Christ Jesus our Lord." Reading the second half of this passage clarifies how God has made a way for us to have freedom from sin and its consequences. It also gives us some insight into why our Creator came and died on the cross. We can gain even more understanding about this by adding one more passage found in the book of John. Jesus said, "For God so loved the world that he gave his one and only Son, that whoever believes in him shall not perish but have eternal life" (John 3:16).

God's plan for rescuing us from ourselves was to come to earth and die on our behalf. Jesus came so we could meet our Creator, but even greater was his intent to pay the penalty of death we had incurred. He made a way for us to be free from the power of sin in our lives, both now and for eternity, allowing us to become the individuals

God created us to be (2 Corinthians 5:21, 1 Peter 2:24, etc.).

When I read these accounts, I come to the realization that I need a Savior in my life. I am not even able to live up to my own standards—much less God's. I need someone who has the power to free me from not only the penalty of my sins but also from their power in my life. I thank God that Jesus fulfilled this role!

The idea that Jesus paid the penalty for your sin and mine can be overwhelming to think about. Yet that is what he did. We are created beings who were not left alone by our Maker, but instead we are loved by him. *The good news is that you have a God who loves you absolutely and completely!*

Our God is actively involved in our lives, and he wants a relationship with us. He is not aloof, uncaring, or incapable. He has an eternal plan for us (Romans 3:23, John 3:16, etc.), and he is carrying it out! Taking our place, Jesus went to the cross on purpose and died the death that we deserve.

Why Wait?

Some have asked me why God allows people to practice evil at the expense of others in this world. Why doesn't he just wipe out evil and those who practice it now? The answer is that he will do this someday (Hebrews 9:27), but until then some insight may be found in the following passage: "The Lord is not slow in keeping his promise, as some understand slowness. He is patient with you, not wanting anyone to perish, but everyone to come to repentance" (2 Peter 3:9).

God loves us and is holding off his judgment until you and I have a chance to respond to him—to receive his free gift of salvation from sin by repenting of our sin and trusting Christ for the finished work he did on the cross for us. Some may feel that they have committed too much evil to deserve this pardon, but we need to understand that none of us deserves this gift; it is a sample of the greatness of our God's love for us. Remember, the verse in 2 Peter says, "Not wanting anyone to perish, but everyone to come to repentance."

Just think about it—the Almighty, the Creator of the universe cares this much about us! We are very fortunate, as he could have been any kind of deity. He could be oppressive, hateful, or even sadistic. He could be dictatorial simply for the sake of being dictatorial. Our Creator could also be uncaring—making us and then leaving us to our own devices.

Yet that is not who he is. He is the God who loves us and waits patiently for us to receive his free gift of salvation from our sin and its consequences. You see, as Creator he holds all of the cards. He has all of the rights, and we have none. We are powerless and voiceless as created beings. But he still chooses to love us and help us, despite the fact that he doesn't have to. He has every right to completely eliminate us and start over with a new race! Instead, he waits patiently for us to become his again.

....

**When we took that gift and used
it to reject and dishonor him,
he still came for us.**

....

God gave us the gift of free will—the ability to choose for ourselves. When we took that gift and used it to reject him and dishonor him, he still came for us. I find this amazing! The Bible describes him as "God our Savior, who wants all men to be saved" (1 Timothy 2:3–4). It also tells us, "But God demonstrates his own love for us in this: While we were still sinners, Christ died for us" (Romans 5:8). While we were still in rebellion against him, while we were still living lives that rejected him, he suffered and died for us to take the punishment we deserved. That's the kind of God we have!

One Way

Jesus said many things that raised the ire of the religious establishment. When Jesus said, "I am the way and the truth and the life. No one comes to the Father except through me" (John 14:6), he was making a truly loaded statement. What was Jesus saying in this passage? Was he being exclusionary, simply wanting to separate himself from other religions?

To understand this statement better, it would be beneficial to consider that it is being spoken by the one who spoke the universe into existence (Colossians 1:16–17). Jesus is the one who healed the sick, gave sight to the blind, and raised people from the dead. He fulfilled prophecies, empowered his disciples, and raised himself from the dead, stating that he would do the same for us in eternity future. What Jesus was saying was that he is our only hope—that he alone has the power to destroy sin and its consequences. What we call religion isn't even in God's equation; it is not part of his plan.

Sin is strong, and it has a grip on our lives in ways that we many times don't even realize. It has changed us into beings that are different than what God created. Only the one who was without sin (2 Corinthians 5:21) has the power to defeat sin in our lives and eventually in the world. The church cannot say it is without sin. No religious person or religious leader can say he or she is without sin. According to Jesus, we need to trust in Christ alone for salvation from sin. He alone is the "way and the truth and the life." He alone is powerful enough.

In the many conversations I've had, I find that people are confused about this and primarily because of what they've been told by religious people, whom they think they can trust. People think they can be free from this sin that kills us by any number of things. Attending church, giving a tithe, getting baptized, going to confession, making a pilgrimage, enduring suffering and trials, becoming members of a church, doing penance, praying a prayer, taking sacraments, completing a missionary journey, doing good deeds, and living right are just some of the reasons I have been given for why someone will end up with God in paradise in the coming age as opposed to hell. Some religions refer to these acts as "good works" or simply "works."

According to Jesus, none of these "ways to salvation" that religion offers will cleanse us of our sin and place us in right standing before our Creator. Only he, God himself, is powerful enough to do this work! It's no wonder we get so confused. God's sacrifice on the cross alone has the ability to free us. It was a powerful work; it was a complete work.

The final words uttered by Jesus on the cross, before he gave his final breath, were, "It is finished" (John 19:30). Jesus was saying that the price was paid, the work was done, and sin had been defeated. Nothing was left for man to do but trust the Son of God for this. Good works and religious acts have no place in God's economy of salvation from sin. Why? Because they have no power. Only the sacrifice of God himself was sufficient and powerful enough.

> And the Lord has laid on him the iniquity of us all. (Isaiah 53:6b)

> For he bore the sins of many, and made intercession for the transgressors. (Isaiah 53:12b)

> He himself bore our sins in his body on the tree, so that we might die to sins and live for righteousness; by his wounds you have been healed. (1 Peter 2:24)

> We have been made holy through the sacrifice of the body of Jesus Christ once

for all … because by one sacrifice he has made perfect forever those who are being made holy … "Their sins and lawless acts I will remember no more." (Hebrews 10:10, 14, 17)

God made him who had no sin to be sin for us, so that in him we might become the righteousness of God. (2 Corinthians 5:21)

But you know that he appeared so that he might take away our sins. (1 John 3:5)

How could we ever think that our good works and religious activities would have the power necessary to change the very core of our nature? That's like taking an aspirin to cure cancer. Trusting in our own deeds is just another way of telling God we're self-sufficient and we don't need him. I place emphasis on all of this because so many I've spoken with misunderstand it. The good news is that our Creator saw our need and met it through the work of Jesus Christ on the cross. He wants us to believe him on this matter. We can trust him for this and have peace. "For it is by grace you have been saved, through faith—and this not from yourselves, it is the gift of God—not by works, so that no one can boast" (Ephesians 2:8–9). We don't have to wonder about our eternal future ever again. If we actively trust God for his gift of salvation through Christ, "We may approach God with freedom and confidence" (Ephesians 3:12).

Good works do have a place and purpose in God's plan for us, though. They are the fruit of a changed life—the natural response of one who has been made a new creation by the power of God (2 Corinthians 5:17). The Bible tells us that a living faith brings about changes and good works in a person, and that the faith of anyone who lacks these is dead, even though they might profess otherwise (James 2:14-26). Good works don't have the power to save us, but they are the evidence of a saving faith. God's Word tells us to still get baptized, to still give tithes, to take communion in fellowship with other believers, to serve others, and to do other good works. These are an expected part of the life of one who has been changed by God.

....

**If God wanted us to love him,
then he needed to set us
free enough to be able to do so.**

....

Some have asked me why God gave us the opportunity to forsake him in the first place. Why did the Almighty give us free will to either accept him or reject him and his sovereignty over his creation? The answer to this is surprisingly simple. He wants a relationship with us. He loves us, but if he made us like robots—with only the ability to obey his every command—then we could never love him in return. If God wanted us to love him, then he needed to set us free enough to be able to do so. He needed to give us the choice of loving him or not. He needed to give us the ability to choose him or reject him, to trust him or dismiss him, to unite with him or live separately from him.

So What Do I Do?

Dear friend, our Creator's desire is for you and me to be free from the bondage of sin—to be slaves to sin and its consequences no more (Romans 6:6). He created each of us to have a purpose. Our lives are to have real meaning from an eternal perspective. "For we are God's workmanship, created in Christ Jesus to do good works, which God prepared in advance for us to do" (Ephesians 2:10).

If you have reached the point of deciding that you need to be rid of sin and its power in this life and the next, and if you want the life of purpose that God created you for, then you may be asking, "What do I do?" Fortunately, God made it simple.

> For God so loved the world that he gave his one and only Son, that whoever believes in him shall not perish but have eternal life. (John 3:16)

> Yet to all who received him, to those who believed in his name, he gave the right to become children of God. (John 1:12)

There are no religious programs to follow and no strange rituals to endure. God wants us to trust him for salvation from sin the same way he wants us to trust him for everything else. We do this by letting him reign as the true King in our lives.

When Jesus began his ministry, he called people to the same thing he calls you and me to today. He tells us to repent (Matthew 4:17). Looking at all that Jesus taught, we learn that repentance is more than simply ceasing sinful acts. When we repent, we tell God that we no longer want to hold the reins to our lives. We then hand those reins over to him. We let him know that our lives are now his to do whatever he wants with, and we trust him with our future here on earth and for all of eternity.

> Then Jesus said to his disciples, "If anyone would come after me, he must deny himself and take up his cross and follow me." (Matthew 16:24)

So once he becomes Master of my life, how do I follow him? Jesus kept it uncomplicated by telling us, "Love the Lord your God with all your heart and with all your soul and with all your mind" and "Love your neighbor as yourself" (Matthew 22:37–39). If we make these two "greatest commandments" our life endeavors, then God will provide each of us with the details and abilities to carry them out. And you will know freedom in a way you never knew or thought possible, despite the circumstances surrounding you.

A Future Judge

Jesus was clear that his first visit to his creation was not for the purpose of judging us but for saving us (John 12:47–48). Many passages of Scripture explain that he will return one day in power, though, to judge all of mankind.

> But the day of the Lord will come like a thief. The heavens will disappear with a roar; the elements will be destroyed by fire, and the earth and everything in it will be laid bare. (2 Peter 3:10)

> But they will have to give account to him who is ready to judge the living and the dead. (1 Peter 4:5)

> For we must all appear before the judgment seat of Christ. (2 Corinthians 5:10)

Each of us must ask ourselves if we are ready for his return, for at that time we will either be counted with those who are his children or numbered among those who are against him.

The moment we trust Jesus with our lives, we become changed. *"Therefore, if anyone is in Christ, he is a new creation; the old has gone, the new has come!"* (2 Corinthians 5:17). We don't become perfect here on earth, but we become cleansed and different in the eyes of our Creator. We cease to be objects of wrath, and we become truly his children for the first time (John 1:12)! Put your trust fully in Christ your Creator today.

> Now fear the Lord and serve him with all faithfulness. Throw away the gods your forefathers worshiped beyond the River and in Egypt, and serve the Lord. But if serving the Lord seems undesirable to you, then choose for yourselves this day whom you will serve, whether the gods your forefathers served beyond the River, or the gods of the Amorites, in whose land you are living. But as for me and my household, we will serve the Lord. (Joshua 24:14–15)

Where Do I Go From Here?

As a new creation in Christ, there are two important things God has for us to do to help us grow. First, start reading the Bible and apply its truths to your life (2 Timothy 2:15, 3:16). This is the only way to understand and experience the full measure of the life God wants you to have. Jesus and his disciples considered the Bible (both the Old Testament and the writings that would become the New Testament) to be God's Word, so we should do the same (Luke 24:25–27, John 10:35, 17:17, 2 Timothy 3:16, 2 Peter 1:21, John 14:26, etc.).

Second, find others who have made the same decision to follow Jesus (Hebrews 10:24–25). The Bible refers to these people as the true church—the body of Christ (Colossians 1:18). Fellowship with these people, serve with these people, encourage these people, and grow with them. God tells us to do these things in his Word because we need them and they need us in order to remain strong and grounded in him.

Pray and ask God to help you find the right church fellowship to grow and serve with, and he will help you with this. Maybe someone gave you this book to read. If so, tell him or her about your decision, and he or she may be able to give you some direction as well.

Tell others the good news of this new life you have in Christ. The Holy Spirit will indwell you and guide you on the most challenging and fulfilling adventure you could ever have. God bless you on your journey!

> Do not let your hearts be troubled. Trust in God; trust also in me. In my Father's house are many rooms; if it were not so, I would have told you. I am going there to prepare a place for you. And if I go and prepare a place for you, I will come back and take you to be with me that you also may be where I am. (John 14:1–7)

> —Jesus Christ

> I write these things to you who believe in the name of the Son of God so that you may know that you have eternal life. (1 John 5:13)

Frequently Asked Questions

Here are a few of the most common questions that have been asked of me through the years. It is my prayer that your questions will be answered, and you will develop the faith to know the Source of all true life.

If Christ is alive, why hasn't he been active on earth for the past two thousand years?

It is certainly understandable why this question has been raised so often, given the never-ending troubles surrounding us in this world. The answer is that Christ has been active, only he's been active in a different way than when he walked among us.

While our God still frequently performs miracles, the greatest work he has been doing is that of healing and transforming people from the inside out instead of the outside in. Jesus said that he will return in power to set things straight and to take his church out of the world. He also said that he would not return until the Bible prophecies concerning the end of the current world order are fulfilled. He even told his disciples some of the signs to watch for (Matthew 24).

During the interim until he returns, Christ is serving as the head of his body, the true church, which is made up of people around us in everyday life who are actively trusting, following, and serving him, and who are also serving others in the process. God the Father uses the power of the Holy Spirit and the power of his Word, the Bible, to draw people to his Son. Daily, people from all backgrounds and nationalities are coming to know the true freedom and life Christ has to offer.

When he returns in the future, Christ will bring an end to all pain, suffering and injustice. Right now, though, the world remains unfair thanks to our sinful, selfish natures. When Adam brought sin into the world (Romans 5:12), creation fell (Romans 8:18-23), and everything we suffer from entered in. Followers of Christ do not escape these problems, but as new creatures we can live victoriously through them. These problems happen to us, but they do not have the power to define us.

Jesus is just as active as ever – let him do his work in you!

....

Isn't the church full of hypocrites?

Taking an initial glance at how the church appears as a whole, my answer to this question would be "yes." But like many things, when we take a closer look our perspectives can change.

Many cities in America and even around the globe have a variety of local Christian churches meeting in them. Within the boundaries of any one city you may find Methodists, Roman Catholics, United Baptists, Lutherans, Byzantine Catholics, Grace Baptists, Anglicans, and Calvinists.

Within any one of these congregations you may find any combination of the following:

1. Those who are mature, active followers of Christ
2. Those who recently became active followers of Christ, but who are still learning. Their behaviors may reflect this.
3. Those who think they are followers of Christ, but aren't. Their behaviors may frequently reflect this.
4. Those who call themselves followers of Christ, but who know they are not. They are knowingly putting up a front to give this false impression to someone, for some reason.
5. Those who are not followers of Christ, and their behaviors may reflect it. They may be at a church service because they are exploring, or they may be there because someone close to them dragged them there, and they may wish they were anywhere else.

Among these five types of churchgoers, only those in categories #1 and #2 are members of the body of Christ, from Christ's perspective. According to Jesus, those who truly trust in him for their lives will also deny themselves, take up their crosses, and follow him (Matthew 16:24). That leaves those in category #3, who are deceived, and those in category #4 who are the true hypocrites by definition. Within any congregation you can potentially find members of Christ's true church coexisting with the counterfeit church. Jesus referred to these two types of people as wheat and tares (Matthew 13:29). He referred to wheat as the desired crop, and to tares as weeds. We can't tell the difference between the two, but he can. This example Jesus used was perfect, and his listeners would have understood perfectly, as tares are a type of weed that looks exactly like wheat. A farmer cannot tell the difference between the two until they reach maturity. Jesus said the two will grow together until the harvest, when he will separate them. He will bring the wheat into his barn, but the tares he will burn (Matthew 13:30).

None of us truly knows what is happening in the heart and life of another person. Even mature, active followers of Christ will make un-Christlike mistakes on occasion. This doesn't make them hypocrites, though. It makes them human, and in need of a savior like Jesus.

Our role is to try not to judge others, but instead to try to build others up and avoid making the same mistakes ourselves. This is a challenging life, and we need each other.

If you are discounting the life-transforming power of Christ due to a few hypocrites, I encourage you to reconsider. Don't allow yourself to miss your eternal destiny because of the behaviors of another. Take a closer look at Jesus' life as recorded in scripture. He is the only one who never failed.

....

You seem to find your proof of God in the Bible – a book that Christians refer to as God's Word. Isn't this circular reasoning?

This is a good question, as I can see how my reasoning can appear this way. I tried to address this issue in chapter 6 of my book. In this chapter, I inform the reader that the primary source of information about Jesus Christ is found in the Bible, and that if we want to learn about his life and teachings we must turn there. Though I used the Bible as this source, I drew on it purely as a historical manuscript – no different than any other historical document.

The Bible contains the writings of Matthew, Mark, Luke, and John. These four followers of Christ each recorded their observations of Jesus' works and his teachings. In addition to these gospel accounts, the Bible includes a number of books containing prophecies about Christ that were spoken hundreds of years before he appeared. It also contains records detailing the power-filled lives of Christ's disciples after he left earth.

The conclusion I draw in my book is that Jesus Christ gives us the proof of a Creator God that I was seeking. Do I believe that the Bible is the written Word of God? Yes – but I treated the Bible purely as a historical document for the purpose of my investigation. Later in the book I reference the Bible as God's Word, but that is after concluding that God exists.

···

There are so many different churches out there – which one should I join?

There is one criteria I use when I decide which church assembly I will be a part of. That criteria is that the pastor and congregation must regard the Bible as the Word of God – teaching it, handling it, and obeying it as such.

I do not want to begin developing my own ideas about who God is and what he wants of me, so I will not join a church family that does that. I want to know God for who he truly is, and I want my life to line up with his plan for it. God gave us information about himself and about his plans for our lives in his Word – the Bible. Here are some verses about God's Word that I find helpful:

- All Scripture is God-breathed and is useful for teaching, rebuking, correcting and training in righteousness, so that the man of God may be thoroughly equipped for every good work. (2 Timothy 3:16-17)
- "Heaven and earth will pass away, but my words will never pass away." (Matthew 24:35)
- Let the word of Christ dwell in you richly... (Colossians 3:16a)
- For the word of God is living and active. Sharper than any double-edged sword, it penetrates even to dividing soul and spirit, joints and marrow; it judges the thoughts and attitudes of the heart. Nothing in all creation is hidden from God's sight. Everything is uncovered and laid bare before the eyes of him to whom we must give account. (Hebrews 4:12-13)

- "There is a judge for the one who rejects me and does not accept my words; that very word which I spoke will condemn him at the last day." (John 12:48)
- "Therefore everyone who hears these words of mine and puts them into practice is like a wise man who built his house on the rock." (Matthew 7:24)
- The grass withers and the flowers fall, but the word of our God stands forever. (Isaiah 40:8)
- How can a young man keep his way pure? By living according to your word. I seek you with all my heart; do not let me stray from your commands. I have hidden your word in my heart that I might not sin against you. (Psalm 119:9-11)
- "Sanctify them by the truth; your word is truth." (John 17:17)

So, when I join a local church, I don't make my decision based on how moving the worship music is, or on how many programs the church has, or on how comfortable the pews and the layout of the building are. My decision is based on God's mandate to place myself under the authority of his written Word so that my life may be directed to accomplish his will and so that my person may be transformed more into Christ's image. This is the point of it all from our Creator's perspective, and it should be the point of it all for each of us as his followers.

But I tried Christ, and nothing happened. Why should I trust him now?

I've been approached by a surprising number of people who have asked me this question. They made decisions to follow Christ at a gospel-preaching crusade that came through town, or at a church rally, or at summer camp as a young person. Somehow, the life that they thought they would have afterward never transpired for them.

Probing this matter deeper with these individuals, I found that some patterns began to develop. In most cases, these folks started out with good intentions. They began reading their Bibles, but gave up after a while when they weren't getting much out of it. They attended a church for a period of time, but stopped when it wasn't meeting their needs. They prayed a fair amount at first, but that slowed down to just occasional prayers when they found their requests weren't being answered the way they hoped.

The consistent theme that appeared the more these individuals shared is that God didn't provide them what they hoped he would. In short, their needs weren't being met. The God, whom they understood as being love, apparently didn't love them.

Friends, our churches are full of people today who are still waiting for God to heap his blessings upon them, and the streets are full of people who will not enter those churches because God has failed them. I don't blame these folks, because in many cases the God who was shared with them is a god created by man. This is a god whose only purpose is to serve us and grant us wishes. This is a god who puts us at the center of the universe.

Of course this god is going to fail us, because he doesn't exist. He is not the God who reveals himself through his Word, the Bible. The God of the Bible – the God of creation loves us so much that he will not meet our every need. In fact, he loves us so much that he will purposely weave hardship into the fabric of our lives (James 1:2-8, Romans 5:3, 1 Peter 4:12, etc.). This is why my one criteria for choosing a church congregation to attend is that they must honor, treat, and apply the Bible as the Word of God.

Don't get me wrong. There are a lot of good pastors and churches out there who preach and teach about the God of the Bible, and they do so accurately. Unfortunately, there are just as many (or more) who teach about the manmade god we just considered.

Jesus did not suffer and die on a cross so that you and I could have the American dream. The American dream is nothing. It is empty and unsatisfying. Sure, it satisfies the flesh, but it does nothing for the soul, and it does nothing to shape us into the beings we were created to be. The life Jesus calls us to is rich beyond measure and entirely transforming. He changes us into new creations at every level of our being. But, it comes at great cost. It cost him everything, and it will cost us everything. Listen to the calling Jesus gives to those who would follow him:

- From that time on Jesus began to preach, "Repent, for the kingdom of heaven is near." (Matthew 4:17)
- "If anyone would come after me, he must deny himself and take up his cross daily and follow me. For whoever wants to save his life will lose it, but

whoever loses his life for me will save it...." (Luke 9:23-24)

- "In the same way, any of you who does not give up everything he has cannot be my disciple." (Luke 14:33)

- "But I tell you, Do not resist an evil person. If someone strikes you on the right cheek, turn to him the other also. And if someone wants to sue you and take your tunic, let him have your cloak as well. If someone forces you to go one mile, go with him two miles. Give to the one who asks you, and do not turn away from the one who wants to borrow from you." (Matthew 5:39-42)

- Then a teacher of the law came to him and said, "Teacher, I will follow you wherever you go." Jesus replied, "Foxes have holes and birds of the air have nests, but the Son of Man has no place to lay his head." Another disciple said to him, "Lord, first let me go and bury my father." But Jesus told him, "Follow me, and let the dead bury their own dead." (Matthew 8:19-22)

- "Anyone who loves his father or mother more than me is not worthy of me; anyone who loves his son or daughter more than me is not worthy of me; and anyone who does not take his cross and follow me is not worthy of me. Whoever finds his life will lose it, and whoever loses his life for my sake will find it." (Matthew 10:37-39)

- Sitting down, Jesus called the Twelve and said, "If anyone wants to be first, he must be the very last, and the servant of all." (Mark 9:35)

- "Go now and leave your life of sin." (John 8:11)

There is nothing easy about the life that Jesus calls us to. It is extreme, but it has to be because the work he wants to do in us is extreme. The only way we can know the fullness of the blessings and life God has for us is to obey the call of Jesus and abandon all else. Otherwise, we will go on thinking that God has not met our needs and has failed us. It becomes a matter of perspective that can't be understood until we surrender ourselves to him.

As I said, there is nothing easy about the life that Jesus calls us to. Because of that, Jesus told the crowds who wanted to follow him to count the cost. (Luke 14:28-32). One of the examples he used is that of someone who started to build a tower, but because they didn't consider the full cost of the tower they ended up having to abandon the project partway through, leaving the tower uncompleted.

Friends, count the cost of following Jesus.... then surrender fully to him and don't let your foot off of the gas pedal until you reach home! Fight against the world's perspectives, your own flesh, and the devil who will all try to get you off track. Remain faithful, remembering that the picture is much bigger than what we see here on earth. You will then come to know the God who does not fail.

Printed in the United States
By Bookmasters